Your Personalized Angel Guide

Introducing Archangels and Angels, and Understanding Who They Are and What Value They Add to Your Life

Dawn Hazel

Dawn Publishing House

© Copyright 2022 - All rights reserved.

The content contained within this book may not be reproduced, duplicated or transmitted without direct written permission from the author or the publisher.

Under no circumstances will any blame or legal responsibility be held against the publisher, or author, for any damages, reparation, or monetary loss due to the information contained within this book, either directly or indirectly.

Legal Notice:

This book is copyright protected. It is only for personal use. You cannot amend, distribute, sell, use, quote or paraphrase any part, or the content within this book, without the consent of the author or publisher.

Disclaimer Notice:

Please note the information contained within this document is for educational and entertainment purposes only. All effort has been executed to present accurate, up to date, reliable, complete information. No warranties of any kind are declared or implied. Readers acknowledge that the author is not engaged in the rendering of legal, financial, medical or professional advice. The content within this book has been derived from various sources. Please consult a licensed professional before attempting any techniques outlined in this book.

By reading this document, the reader agrees that under no circumstances is the author responsible for any losses, direct or indirect, that are incurred as a result of the use of the information contained within this document, including, but not limited to, errors, omissions, or inaccuracies.

Table of Contents

INTRODUCTION 1
   MEETING ANGELS 3
      Earth Angels 4
      Heavenly Angels 5
   LET THE EXPEDITION BEGIN 7
CHAPTER 1: CELESTIAL HIERARCHY: THE ORDER OF THE ANGELS 9
   UNDERSTANDING THE CELESTIAL SPHERES 10
      First Sphere 11
         Seraphim 11
         Cherubim 13
         Thrones 14
      Second Sphere 15
         Dominions 15
         Virtues 16
         Powers 17
      Third Sphere 17
         Principalities 18
         Archangels 18
         Angels 19
CHAPTER 2: ANGEL INTERACTIONS 21
   YOU ARE NEVER ALONE 22
   HOW ARE ANGELS TRYING TO COMMUNICATE WITH YOU? 23
      Dreams 24
      Temperature Changes 25
      Visual Communication 25
      Feathers 27
      Numbers 28
      Other Examples 28
   ANGEL CALLING CARDS 29
      Finding Misplaced Items 30
      Coping With Changes 31
      Financial Assistance 31
      Other Examples 32
   HOW TO ACTIVATE ANGEL CALLING CARDS 33
      Writing 33
      Performing Arts 34

  Verbal Communication *34*
  Meditation *34*
  In Conclusion *35*
THE ANGEL GUIDEINTRODUCTION TO THE ANGEL GUIDE................**37**
 Archangels.. 41
  Archangel Michael *42*
  Archangel Raphael *44*
  Archangel Gabriel *47*
  Archangel Jophiel *48*
  Archangel Ariel *50*
  Archangel Azrael *51*
  Archangel Chamuel *53*
  Archangel Barachiel *54*
  Archangel Haniel *55*
  Archangel Israfel *56*
  Archangel Jeremiel *57*
  Archangel Metatron *58*
  Archangel Raguel *59*
  Archangel Raziel *61*
  Archangel Sandalphon *62*
  Archangel Uriel *64*
  Archangel Zadkiel *65*
 In Summary 66
ANGELS **69**
 Meeting Your Angels 71
  Angel Achaiah *72*
  Angel Aladiah *72*
  Angel Amatiel *73*
  Angel Amitiel *74*
  Angel Anachel *75*
  Angel Anauel *75*
  Angel Aniel *76*
  Angel Asaliah *77*
  Angel Cassiel *78*
  Angel Cahetel *79*
  Angel Caliel *80*
  Angel Chavaquiah *80*
  Angel Damabiah *81*
  Angel Daniel *83*
  Angel Dokiel *83*
  Angel Elemiah *84*
  Angel Eyael *85*

- Angel Muriel 86
- Angel Nathaniel 88
- Angel Ramaela... 89
- Angel Sachiel... 90

FALLEN ANGELS 92

My Understanding of Fallen Angels 93
Meeting the Fallen Angels 94
- The Devil 96
  - The Former Angel 97
- Moloch 98
- Chemosh 99
- Dagon 100
- Belial 102
- Beelzebub.. 104

.CONCLUSION 106

Honestly Asked and Answered 108
- Are Angels Real? 108
- What Leads You to Believe that Angels are Real? 108
- Do You Believe in Angels? 109
- Why Do You Believe in Angels? 109
- Are Angels Important to Your Daily life?... 109
- What Leads You to Believe in the Importance of Angels?................... 109

A Message of Hope and Encouragement 111

REFERENCES 113

Image References 126

Introduction

- Are angels real?
- What leads you to believe that angels are real?
- Do you believe in angels?
- Why do you believe in angels?
- Are angels important to your daily life?
- What leads you to believe in the importance of angels?
- What roles do angels portray in our daily lives?

I like to believe that angels are real and that they are guiding me as I navigate through the maze of life. I may find myself being the only person in a room, but yet I feel as though I am not alone. Friends and family have shared their angel encounters with me, and it is for this reason that I have decided to explore these experiences.

I am exhausted by all the negativity that surrounds me whenever I open my eyes, speak, or listen to what is going on. I am not oblivious to what is going on in the world, but the time has come to focus on happy and positive experiences. It is up to each of us to create those experiences and the best place to start would be looking at the angels who accompany us throughout life. We can't see the angels because they are hidden beneath a cloak of invisibility, but their presence is felt.

Angels are appointed by God to act as His messengers and ambassadors. They are heavenly spiritual beings that do not have physical bodies. Angels will be presented to us in any way, shape, or form such as winged creatures or by light displays. You don't have to be a Christian to believe in angels. I understand that religion is a touchy subject for many, especially in the face of grief or trials and tribulations. Having something to believe in during these difficult times, however, helps people cope with the circumstances.

Meeting Angels

What would you say if I told you that you have probably come face-to-face with an angel? We have heaven-bound angels who are hidden from our sight and are hidden beneath their invisibility cloaks. We also have "earth angels" who are regular human beings like you and me. In a way, we are angels, especially when we have a prompting to do good in the world such as helping someone in need, sharing a friendly smile, or saying something kind to someone else. I like to believe that earth angels have taken the shape of Good Samaritans who have passed through our lives and left their footprints behind. Still not a believer? Let's take a look to see if you have encountered an earth angel and didn't realize it.

Earth Angels

Your heart and mind are filled with dark thoughts. You feel as if you will never find the light again. Your dark thoughts threaten your existence, but a source of bright light enters your dark chambers. You don't feel judged or condemned by this person as you would if it were someone you were close to. You share what is in your heart and your healing begins. Your dark chamber becomes lighter and brighter as your healing progresses.

You have reached a stage in your life where you feel worthless and unappreciated. You feel as if you are running on autopilot and everything, from chores to work assignments, seems laborious. In short, you have run out of steam. But then, you are either driving along or you are at the grocery store, and someone smiles at you. Your first reaction is to look around because, why would a stranger be smiling at you? There is no one, other than you and the smiling stranger, in the aisle. You smile back and without realizing it, you have been touched by a gesture of kindness from a stranger.

Personal experience has led me to believe that earth angels have a magic power that makes us think about where we are in our life journey. We are so busy rushing around to get everything done that we often neglect ourselves. We don't realize just how much we carry around with us until someone cool, calm, and collected enters our lives. All the panic and stress about getting everything done goes out the window when an earth angel enters our proximity. They allow us to slow down and appreciate our surroundings, as well as the people in our lives. Who can go from stress and panic to cool as a cucumber in a matter of moments?

Have you ever been in a situation where you are holding onto something that is weighing you down? Have you ever known or done something, but you can't share it with anyone? Again, fear of judgment or condemnation keeps you rooted to the spot. You may be having lunch at the park and someone sits near you. You smile at each other. You greet each other. You go back into your weighted spot. A little sigh or a groan escapes through your lips without you realizing it. The stranger asks if you are okay and that is the opening you need to unpack your baggage. You may just find that the chance encounter was something that you both needed.

It doesn't matter what you are going through in your life, there will always be someone who will enter your life to provide you with assistance. Stand in front of your mirror and ask yourself if you are an earth angel. Think carefully before answering that question and think about what you may or may not have done for people in your life or perfect strangers. I do believe that each of us are earth angels. Some of us may have a harder exterior than others, but when it comes to being there for others, we will step up to the plate.

Heavenly Angels

This book is about angels and whether they are real or not. And more specifically, heavenly angels—who as I have already mentioned, are created by God and act as messengers and ambassadors. We are not going to start a debate about whether angels are mythical beings or not. We are not going to argue about religion. This is an open-opinion guide about angels and the roles they portray in our worldly lives.

We appeal to God or whichever deity we believe in for assistance without realizing it. We beg for enlightenment, courage, or wisdom. God sees all. He has his hand on everything. It is for this reason that it makes sense that He has heavenly helpers. The heavenly helpers were hand-picked by Him and his Son to be of help to everyone. The angels don't act on their own, but they do act on the guidance of God. The prayers and cries for help are not only handled by God on those heavenly support hotlines.

How many times do you think the word 'angels' is mentioned in the Bible? Would you believe me if I said they are mentioned 273 times? I would like to share some interesting facts with you regarding angels as we prepare for our journey through angel territory.

- Angels don't die—Luke 20:36
- Angels lived before God created the earth—Job 38:1-7
- Angels are single and will not get married to reproduce—Matthew 22:30
- Angels are intelligent—Daniel 9:22
- Angels have an interest in what happens in our daily lives—Daniel 10:14 and Luke 15:10
- Angels are spiritual beings and not mythical creatures—Psalm 104:4
- Angels should not be worshiped like false idols—Revelation 19:10
- Angels answer to God—1 Peter 3:22, Job 1:6, and Job 2:1
- Angels are emotional—Job 38:7
- Most angels are faithful to God—Revelation 5:11-12

Angels are also known as messengers, military hosts, chariots, and Sons of God (Fairchild, 2020).

Let the Expedition Begin

We have gathered here, at this spot, to take the next steps together. I am going to be your tour guide as we set out on our journey. I am going to introduce you to the different types of angels and their orders that form part of the celestial hierarchy. At no point will you be asked to pay for anything, nor will you be directed to sign up for any subscriptions. You will not be judged or bullied at any point during this journey. I want you to be comfortable at all times. It doesn't matter if you don't believe in angels at this moment in time, but I would like you to enter into this expedition with an open mind and to be prepared for the unexpected.

- Are you ready?
- Are you dressed comfortably?
- Do you have a flask of hot chocolate, coffee, tea, or water?
- Do you have a bowl of snacks?

Let's get our feet in the sand and create some positive and happy footprints so that we can enrich the lives of others with what the angels are going to reveal to us throughout this book.

Chapter 1:
Celestial Hierarchy: The Order of the Angels

Have you ever taken a step back and looked at where you are? Where are you and how do you rank in the current chain of order in your life? I have never thought much about it because I always went with the flow. The research I have been conducting for my Angel Guide has sparked an interest in the chain of succession in the celestial world. I find myself comparing the ranks and types of angels to my life and those of the people around me. I have realized that thanks to Matthew 6:10; "as it is in heaven, so it is on earth."

Take a look at yourself. You entered this world as a baby. What happens then? You go through the various stages of being a toddler, a teenager, an adult, and then an elderly person. You are making a way for others as you progress through the stages of life. Let's take a look at the corporate world. You start at the bottom of the company doing mundane tasks. Your supervisors notice you and the hard work you do and you get a promotion. You will climb the ladder of success until you cannot go any further.

I would like to point out that while we have to go through the stages of life or business (whether we like it or not), it is something that has to happen. You may be going through the stages, but no one is more superior than the next person. A baby can't speak and spends most of its time eating and sleeping. Is the baby less significant than the toddler who can string together a couple of words and get into mischief? Absolutely not. Everyone, no matter who or where you are, plays an important role in the lives of those they come in contact with.

Understanding the Celestial Spheres

I am not oblivious to the fact that non-believers are walking with us, and some may even live with you. I am not in the position to judge people for their choices, nor would I want to. Everyone believes in someone or something and it is not up to you or me to change their way of thinking. Christians know that God sits on the highest throne. He can see all the corners of the earth from his vantage point. God sees all, hears all, and—rumor has it—He knows what we are thinking because we think it.

As I mentioned in the introduction, God may have His hand on everything that is happening on earth but even He needs a helping hand. Let's take a closer look at the celestial hierarchy. I am going to introduce you to the three tiers (or spheres) that make up the celestial ladder of angels. Each of the tiers has three types of angels. It is important to know, as I touched on previously, that it does not matter in which tier the angels fall under—each angel is special, unique, and portrays an important role in their line of succession.

Let's explore the three tiers of the celestial hierarchy. I want us to have an understanding of everything that happens on the operational side of all things related to angels. We are going to soak up all the knowledge at our disposal and carry what we have learned forward when we are introduced to the angels in our Angel Guide.

First Sphere

The first sphere is believed to be the highest level within the celestial hierarchy. The angels that take up residence in this first sphere are the direct servants or advisors to God. They are also the furthest away from earth, but are closest to God in heaven. The angels in the first sphere will communicate with the other angels in an advisory position to relay messages to those of us living on earth. The first sphere of the celestial hierarchy houses three types of angels.

Seraphim

The top position within the celestial hierarchy belongs to the highest-ranking angels, namely seraphim. These fiery celestial spiritual beings are the most important types of angels within the first sphere. Seraphim is the plural of seraph because we all know that there is strength in numbers, and why stop at one angel when you can have a whole host? Multiple theology publications and online blog posts mention that Seraphim are directly in contact with God, and they are eager and burning to serve Him. The Seraphim have an intense love for God; the love is so intense that they want to spend all their time in praise and worship to Him. Seraphim hold God's name in the highest as they serve Him. They are also the direct line of communication when messages need to be passed along to the lower-ranking angels.

The Seraphim are a vision of glory and beauty according to Isaiah. He shares his encounter with the Lord, and of the angels who are closely surrounding Him. I am certain that if you close your eyes and envision the scene as described in Isaiah 6:1–8, you too will see a vivid image of the loving Seraphim as they surround God. Isaiah 6:2 says: "Above him were seraphim, each with six wings: With two wings they covered their faces, with two they covered their feet, and with two they were flying." Isaiah 6:6–7 says: "Then one of the seraphim flew to me with a live coal in his hand, which he had taken with tongs from the altar. With it he touched my mouth and said, 'See, this has touched your lips; your guilt is taken away and your sin atoned for.'"

Cherubim

The second spot in the line of succession belongs to the Cherubim. These angels have been misrepresented over the decades due to art images that represent chubby little angels that look like babies with little wings. Cherubim is the plural for cherubs; because again, why have only one cherub when you can have a little army of Cherubim?

Cherubim are mentioned numerous times in the Bible. The first time the cherubim is mentioned is in Genesis 3:24; "After he drove the man out, he placed on the east side of the Garden of Eden cherubim and a flaming sword flashing back and forth to guard the way to the tree of life." What this verse is telling us is that God made the Cherubim guardians of the Garden of Eden. Their role was to protect the tree of knowledge after Adam and Eve were told to leave and never return.

So, we know what their roles are but what we don't know is what their appearance is. We have already learned that the visual representations we see in paintings and sculptures are wholly inaccurate. And judging by the snippet of information from the Book of Genesis, we can clearly see that they are anything but chubby little cherubs flying around. Ezekiel 1:5–11 gives the best description of Cherubim. Ezekiel 1:10–11 says: "Their faces looked like this: Each of the four had the face of a human being, and on the right side each had the face of a lion, and on the left the face of an ox; each also had the face of an eagle. Such were their faces. They each had two wings spreading out upward, each wing touching that of the creature on either side; and each had two other wings covering its body."

Thrones

The third and final angels in the first sphere belong to the Thrones. The Thrones are not referenced in the Bible as vividly and as frequently as the Seraphim and the Cherubim, but that doesn't mean that they don't play an important role in the celestial hierarchy. The Thrones are believed to be living symbols of God's justice.

These angels go on missions to help restore the imbalance that is harmful to the universe. The Thrones are tasked with upholding God's laws, which also means conveying God's will about justice and judicial power. These messages are communicated to the lower-ranking angels who are then tasked with spreading the warnings to us on earth. Likewise, if lower-ranking angels need to get messages to God, they will have to go through the Thrones as the first sphere is protective of Him.

Though the Bible doesn't go into as much detail about the Thrones, I did manage to find three references which I believe give us a glimpse of what to expect should we ever try to find our way into the first sphere. Daniel 7:9 says: "As I looked, thrones were set in place, and the Ancient of Days took his seat. His clothing was as white as snow; the hair of his head was white like wool. His throne was flaming with fire, and its wheels were all ablaze." Colossians 1:16 adds: "For in him all things were created: things in heaven and on earth, visible and invisible, whether thrones or powers or rulers or authorities; all things have been created through him and for him." Ezekiel 1:15–18 gives us the only description of what the Thrones look like: "As I looked at the living creatures, I saw a wheel on the ground beside each creature with its four faces. This was the appearance and structure of the wheels: They sparkled like topaz, and all four looked alike. Each appeared to be made like a wheel intersecting a wheel. As they moved, they would go in any one of the four directions the creatures faced; the wheels did not change direction as the creatures went. Their rims were high and awesome, and all four rims were full of eyes all around." The four faces that are being referred to in these verses are about the Cherubim but the intersecting wheels with eyes are referring to the Thrones.

Second Sphere

Now we know that the first sphere angels are in direct contact with God. They are God's messengers and their position is to serve, worship, and adore Him. The first sphere angels are his protectors or shields; they are the ones who act as mediators and convey messages from God. We know that the first sphere is protected, and in a way, the angels in the second sphere are enforcing that protection rule.

The second sphere angels can be seen as heavenly governors. Everyone has to have a supervisor to keep the workplace running like a well-oiled machine. This is the task that the second sphere group of angels is entrusted with. They offer support and guidance to ensure that the throne of God does not fail at the hands of inefficiency. Let's meet the next group of angels that form part of the celestial hierarchy.

Dominions

The first group of angels in the second sphere is known as the Dominions. These angels do not have direct contact with God, but they do receive their messages via the Seraphim, Cherubim, or the Thrones. It is then their job to communicate with the lower-ranking angels to pass along the messages and tasks from God. Dominions might not have direct contact with earthlings, but they are high in authority and power over us.

Zadkiel, whom we will meet in our Angel Guide, is believed to be the leader of the Dominions. I could not find any direct references in the Bible that give us a biblical description of Dominions. My research, however, took me to various online publications that share their interpretation. It is believed that the Dominions are the most exquisite-looking and human-like angels, with a single pair of wings. Their beauty may have been captured accurately by numerous artists, but let's not forget to add that the Dominions are believed to carry around scepters or swords as well that feature orbs of light (Baines, n.d.).

Virtues

The Virtues occupy the second spot in the second sphere of the celestial hierarchy. I believe that the Virtues are where everything regarding angels and our beliefs start coming together. The Virtues are also known as the 'Strongholds' because of the power that they are entrusted with. Their duties include encouraging us to be strong in our faith by inspiring people who struggle in their lives and to help them grow in their spirituality. Humans are not meant to see angels, but more often than not we do feel their presence.

The Virtues are believed to visit earth to perform tasks on behalf of God from time to time. God will empower the Virtues to answer prayer requests or perform miracles. The Virtues sit on their heavenly perches in the second sphere to keep an eye out for the world that God created. They also keep a very close eye on the balance between good and bad in our lives. I guess we could argue that the Virtues are the voice of reason when we need to make a right or wrong decision, and how each decision will affect us. The Virtues also have to keep the lower-ranking angels busy by delegating tasks and messages that have been handed down by the first sphere angels.

Powers

In the third and final spot, and thereby blocking the entry point to the second sphere, we have the Powers. This group of celestial beings is also known as Warrior Angels or Authorities because of the amount of power they hold within their ranks in the hierarchy. These angels are pretty special in the greater realm of the universe. It is in their job description to protect the heavens and the earth against evil. They have the power to stand up against the devil and resist the attacks of the demons. It is painfully obvious that not all attacks against us are thwarted by the Powers. It is up to us to join the battle of good and evil as well. You can be equipped with all the tools needed to fight a battle, but you have to use those tools and not dismiss them.

Let's take a look at a likely scenario where the Powers will be part of your life. You are overcome with anger. It is so intense that you want to say something or you may want to pummel someone's face because you didn't like what was said or done. The anger radiates a heat deep within your soul. The heat keeps rising as the offender keeps spewing words that do not meet your approval. Out of nowhere, you feel the temperature starting to reduce. Your soul starts settling. The urge to react in anger starts fading. That, my friends, are the Powers taking over the spiritual battle so that you don't become a victim to the evil attempt of tarnishing your spirituality. Not everyone will surrender their anger to the Powers, but it doesn't mean that they aren't there taking the brunt of the attack.

Third Sphere

We have made it to the third and final sphere in the celestial hierarchy. It really doesn't matter in which sphere the angels fall. I have mentioned previously that there is nothing shameful about not being in the top spot. I have a vivid imagination when it comes to hierarchy, and I like to believe that the angels don't care where they fall within the chain of command. All that matters to them is that they want to help God, are eager to guide us, to protect us, and to do everything they can to spread positivity in the lives of people they come in contact with.

The angels that find themselves in the third sphere are rather special in that they are closer to the earth. That means that they are closer to us. They are also the first responders when we call on angels for help. Do keep in mind that they act as messengers for God and they are in charge of justice and authority. Let's meet the last group of angels that bring up the rear of the celestial hierarchy.

In all honesty, I am inclined to favor the angels in this sphere. I might not see them, but I know that I can look out for special signs, messages, or savor the angelic calmness I will feel. It is also a wonderful idea to know that I can call out for help when I'm feeling troubled. I know that God will give the angels the message I am desperately waiting for.

Principalities

The first angels in the third sphere are called Principalities angels, or Rulers. These angels have a pretty big job in their sphere, which is to protect groups of people or large institutions which include churches, countries, and towns. Principalities have the authority to dictate the will of God to the angel groups below them, as well as give them orders and tasks of missions they need to fulfill. Principalities angels guide and encourage us to pray and develop disciplines within our spirituality to draw us closer to God. Another reason why these angels are so amazing is that they are part of the lower-ranking angels that help us see messages.

Archangels

Don't let the second to last ranking in the last sphere of the celestial hierarchy distract your view of archangels. Everyone, regardless of religion or lack thereof, has heard about archangels. It would be easy to find yourself in a heated argument with someone who insists that archangels are the highest-ranking angels across the three spheres. The Merriam-Webster online dictionary tells us that the definition of archangel means "Chief Angel" (Merriam-Webster, n.d.).

The research I have done has led me around in circles. While one group says that there was only one archangel, another says that there are three; and then when you look at Judaism, they claim that there are seven archangels. Who is right? Who is wrong? Well, I turned to my trusty research partner, the Bible, for guidance. When you look at 1 Thessalonians 4:16 it says: "For the Lord himself will come down from heaven, with a loud command, with the voice of the archangel and with the trumpet call of God, and the dead in Christ will rise first." When reading the verse a couple of times, it is evident that the scripture refers to one archangel in the singular form. Could that be an indication that there is only one and not multiple archangels?

At the end of the day, it doesn't matter how many archangels there are because the only thing that matters is that they are messengers from God. They are here to guide us and protect us. Let's agree that in all honesty, the world we live in has enough going on and it is time that we all take a step back and absorb the messages, visions, and tasks that the archangels send our way. It is time to make our world a happier place again. Are you going to join me?

Angels

Angels (or Guardian Angels) occupy the last spot in the third sphere of the celestial hierarchy. This group of celestial beings are the furthest from God but are closest to us on earth. We have learned that the third sphere group of angels are messengers from God. They are handed tasks that they need to fulfill, so I am not going to go ahead and repeat everything that has already been discussed.

I would, however, like to share something I heard during my research. A lady I spoke to told me about an incident where you can only believe that Angels are real. A friend of the lady's father was in the hospital during the height of the pandemic. He was undergoing multiple tests to find the cause of his heart condition. The lady prayed for her friend's father. She explained the intensity of the prayer and how she felt as if she was on fire. The prayer included the members of their family, and most importantly for the father. Sadly, the friend's father passed away and the lady found herself doubting her faith.

It wasn't until a couple of weeks later when she was speaking to her neighbor that she was told about the "glowing robed figure with hands held high." The lady knew exactly when this had happened. The anger and resentment she had in her melted away. She realized that God had His reasons for taking her friend's father. The angel had come to prepare the lady for the realization that her friend's father wasn't going to be returning. These are the types of messages we need to understand when it comes to interpreting what the angels and God give us.

Chapter 2:

Angel Interactions

Chapter 1 took us on an expedition where we explored the celestial hierarchy. We uncovered some pretty interesting information that relates to the different types of angels and their roles in heaven. Were you aware of the different spheres or tiers before reading this book? Did you know about the different types of angels? There is no shame in admitting that you didn't know about the tiers or about the roles the angels play in heaven and on earth. I am learning about these things right here with you. I'm not ashamed of my lack of knowledge because it is allowing me to grow in my spirituality. The research and interaction with the people I have met during this phase have made it possible to share my knowledge with everyone.

I have seen multiple stories taken from real-life events that have been twisted and turned to make it look as if the event was a once-in-a-lifetime miracle or tragedy. The Internet can be a wonderful source of information, but it can also be a source of deception. I would caution you to do some fact-checking before believing everything you see or hear. Shows such as *Highway to Heaven* (1984–1989) and *Touched by an Angel* (1994–2003) took us on weekly angelic excursions. Each week you were introduced to people from different walks of life who were struggling with something that was holding them back. The angels entered their lives without revealing their true identities and helped them. At the end of each episode, the angels revealed their true identities and shared their purpose for being there at that time.

Hollywood also helped in bringing the angels to the big screens by releasing movies such as *The Bishop's Wife* which features the late Cary Grant, Loretta Young, David Niven (1947). This movie was then remade and renamed *The Preacher's Wife* which stars Denzel Washington and the late Whitney Houston (1996). *City of Angels* was another movie that stars Nicholas Cage and Meg Ryan (1998), there was also *Little*

Nicky featuring Adam Sandler (2000), and many more involving angels and fallen angels that span the genres of drama, comedy, or suspense.

You Are Never Alone

- Have you ever heard the phrase, "if you need anything, please ask"?
- Have you ever tried to reach out for help only to be ignored or encounter a wall of excuses?
- Have you ever needed a kind hand or a caring ear during a difficult time in your life?
- Have you ever felt frustrated or betrayed by people who expect you to jump when they ask for help, but then everything is too much trouble for them to return the favor?
- Do you believe that you are alone all the time?

Raise your hand if you have answered 'yes' to one or all of these questions. I know how infuriated these situations make you feel. You don't need my reassurance, but I can tell you that the resentment that builds up inside of you is not going to help you. Your perception of the situation may be obscured by your distrust, and I can tell you that it is nothing to be or feel ashamed about. I don't know what is happening in your life and I can't speak for anyone else, but I want you to know that even though you believe that you are alone, you never truly are.

You know that this book is about angels and the roles they play in our lives. You may even argue that you don't believe in angels, or that you are not a spiritual or religious person. I'm not about to judge you for your choices, but I would like you to read through this chapter with an open mind. Let down your guard a little and think about the examples I am going to share with you in this section. I may be presumptuous, but I believe that your blurred vision will begin to clear as you realize that you are not as alone as you think you are.

How Are Angels Trying to Communicate With You?

Human beings develop the gene of skepticism when they enter adulthood. I have heard people around me say that they would give up being adults if they can go back to being carefree kids again. They wouldn't have to carry around the weight of being adults who have to work to earn money to keep a roof over their heads, food in their stomachs, and gas in their cars. You struggle to define whether the bag of groceries or the gas gift card was given with pure intentions or if someone will come and reclaim the gifts at a later stage. It is difficult for you to believe that there are good people who want to make your life easier. I get that because I have been in that position and so have billions of others.

The time has come to change your way of thinking. It is time to accept that people come and go from our lives for a reason. I know it is easier to build a protective wall around yourself, but at the end of the day you are missing out on wonderful opportunities. Yes, I am referring to angels that want to comfort you when you are sad, want to calm you down when you feel a wave of burning anger, or who want to help you when you need help. It is time to start etching away at your protective exterior. Drop some of the weight you are carrying around (and I'm not talking about the extra pounds that have crept up over the years). I want nothing more than for you to experience a freedom that has been lost to you for so long.

Let's take a look at some of the signs you may have missed or ignored that indicate that the angels have been trying to communicate with you. I must also add, angels are relentless and they don't give up on us. Remember that their tasks and missions come from the very top sphere of the celestial hierarchy. Those tasks are sent down the ladder to reach the worker angels who live to see a mission completed. Don't be afraid of your angels. Open your mind and allow them to reach out a helping hand.

Dreams

Regardless of age, gender, or religion, everyone dreams—including animals. Most times you can't remember what you dreamt about and other times you remember the dream as if it happened in real-time. The stories or picture books are being created by your active mind. Some dreams make sense and play out the way you want them to, while others leave you confused. Dreams can evoke all types of emotions such as happiness, sadness, or fear.

Angels have many ways of making contact with humans, and one of the most popular ways is visiting you in your dreams. I know it sounds a little stalkerish to think that angels can enter your subconscious state of mind whenever they want. They can be pretty persistent when it comes to getting their messages across, especially when all other methods of communication have failed.

Angels will bring you messages by way of recurring dreams for however long it takes you to realize that you have been *angeled*. Dreams are not limited to stories, they can also include themes or visual images. People have been known to have premonition dreams where they wake up with a vision of their future and what may be waiting for them whether it is good or bad. Angel dreams are not meant to scare you or intimidate you. They are, however, meant to help you make decisions that will positively affect your life. You don't have to listen to your angels, but then don't complain about having the same dream every night for the next couple of months.

Temperature Changes

Skeptics would tell you that the temperature changes have to do with the climate you are living in. If you are in the grips of summer where the temperatures reach between 90°F to 104°F, you would normally associate a sudden chill with air coming from the fridge, freezer, or air conditioner. There is only one problem, and that is when you are alone at home, in the office, or driving in your car and you feel a sudden chill. The hair on your arms and the back of your neck stand to attention, and you experience goosebumps all over your body. Either you are in for a severe virus and you should probably head home and start drinking chicken noodle soup, or your angel is trying to get your attention.

Retrace your thought process if and when you experience any form of unexplainable changes in temperatures or weather disturbances that only you can see. You may not realize that you are thinking about anything specific but one thing is certain—your angel is one smart cookie and can pick up on any trigger word that you may have thought of. You'd do well to listen and take on any of the hints they are dropping on your goosebumps or arm and neck hairs.

Visual Communication

I am not going to tell you that you will, without a doubt, see an angel. Yes, people have mentioned that they have seen angels (refer to Chapter 1) and no, there is nothing wrong with you if you don't or have never encountered one. However, you may have had a couple of encounters that you didn't know were your angel watching over you, or trying to guide you through some pretty dense mazes. Angels will always be there for you, and it doesn't matter where you are in your spiritual journey. They will continue entertaining you until you let down your walls and believe that they are there for you.

Visual signs of communication come in various shapes and sizes. Some people have mentioned seeing colorful orbs floating around a room. Skeptics may argue that the orbs are because of the way one light meets another. An argument in response will be that there are no lights on in the room and that the person witnessing these orbs is alone at the home. Another example would be that you saw a flash of light from the corner of your eye while you were focusing on reading, knitting, crocheting, or watching television. I can't think of a better way to grab hold of my attention to let me know that angels are trying to communicate with me. And, I have to say that I do rather love a pretty light show whether it be colorful orbs, sudden bursts of light flashes, or any swirling lights because then I know that I am not alone.

Feathers

I have spoken to many people who have shared their experience with finding feathers in random places. I have heard about feathers landing on people when there is not a breath of wind and no one else around them. This is a sign that fascinates me because I have had feathers, especially white ones, cross my path without any notice.

It is believed that feather sightings are signs that angels are present. Feather sightings are also linked to people who are grieving the loss of loved ones or friends who have passed on. The angels are letting people know that they are loved, protected, and everything will be good. You may want to collect your feathers and start a scrapbook so that you have them all together as a reminder that you are loved and protected at all times.

You may not only want to keep your focus on physical feathers, but also look for logos or symbols around you. It could be a cloud that has taken the shape of wings where feathers come from, logos on the clothing you wear, or on signboards in stores or along the freeway. These interactions may take place during a vulnerable period in your life which would be an indication that your angel is protecting you and enveloping you with love.

Numbers

Another type of interaction that is frequently ignored is the sighting of numbers. They happen to fall into the category of "now that you know about it, you can't ignore it." I believe that angels want you to think about what you are seeing. They will leave you messages or signs that don't make sense, but the moment it keeps crossing your line of vision or range of hearing, you will start connecting the dots. What you may have thought was a coincidence—seeing the same numbers or the same sequence of numbers—might tickle your curiosity to do some independent research. That research reveals that you are receiving messages from your angels.

Seeing numbers holds a very special place in my heart. It is so special that I wrote a book about it titled, *Angel Numbers 1–9 Meaning: How To Understand the Divine Messages Angels Are Showing You for Twin Flames, Grief, Love, Change, Lost Loved Ones, Friends*. It will already have been published on Amazon by the time this book is released. The fascination I have with all things angel-related is what prompted me to explore the angelic atmosphere.

Other Examples

The angel interactions don't stop here and the lists can go on for days. The most important piece of information to remember is that you are not, and you will never be, alone. There will always be someone or something with you. I would like to leave you with a list of possible signs to look out for before we move on to the next section of this chapter. Remember to have an open mind and don't be afraid to look for those signs. You may just find some healing power knowing that you have angels surrounding you.

- A persistent ringing in your ears could be an angel trying to talk to you.
- The sudden appearance of a rainbow will either point you in the right direction or let you know that you are loved.
- The sighting of butterflies or dragonflies is your angels letting you know that they are nearby.
- The feeling that someone is watching you even though you are sitting in a room with the curtains drawn may just be your angels letting you know that you can lean on them for support.
- You may wake up one morning to find friends or influencers on social media who are posting meaningful messages which may be your angel letting you know that they see you and they are there for you when you are ready for help.
- Good Samaritans crossing your path to brighten your day may be your angels sending you the help you have been yearning for during your silent battles.

Angel Calling Cards

Your mind is partially open to the idea that angels are trying to communicate with you. The other part of your mind is guarded because you are afraid to have hope. I have given you examples of ways in which angels are trying to let you know that they are seeing and hearing your silent calls for help. You may be shaking your head in denial because you have never asked for help, whether it be verbally or nonverbally. That is the beauty of the angels.

If you take a quick time hop back to Chapter 1, you may recall that I mentioned that God knows what we are thinking before we think it.

He knows about the silent battles we fight and the hurt we try to bury. It doesn't matter whether you believe God is real or not, He will never forsake you. No matter what, He is your creator and He will continue to send you messages through the spheres. The angels will always be there for you—even if you don't believe in them. That is how much you are loved and cared for in the celestial hierarchy.

Okay, it is time to put your skepticism on the back burner for a moment or two. I would like you to join me as we take a look at some of the reasons that may prompt us to call on angels. I want you to keep in mind that you can call on the angels to assist with any situation, problem, or need you may have. Please be advised that patience is needed when you ask for assistance or guidance, and you need to work with the angels to achieve the desired results. You don't have to pay the angels for their work other than acknowledge them with thanks. The telephone and internet lines are not currently available in the spheres, but I am pretty confident that their Boss may like to hear from you by way of verbal communication how your angels performed.

Finding Misplaced Items

I can't tell you how many times I have 'lost' something and spent hours and days rummaging through cupboards and drawers looking for it. You know your item is in a specific place but when you want it again, it has grown little feet and wandered off. You retrace your steps and mentally go through the motions only to return to the scene of the crime to find it still empty. You become overwhelmed as frustration and mild panic start setting in. Your emotions are heightened because you *need* to find *that* item. Desperation leads you to cry out for help; "Where are you item?!"

Calmness washes over you and you head off to the kitchen to make a cup of coffee. Your mind is still actively thinking about which cupboard or room you should be rummaging through next. Your roaming eye is scanning the room (and the scene of the crime) from a distance when...Wait! What? How? Could it be? You see the item in a spot not too far from where you last saw it. You had been turning that space upside down more times than you care to admit (the destruction is evident). How could you have missed it? How did it get there?

Well, in a way you asked for help. You wanted to know where the item was. Your angel suggested you take a break. The break allowed your mind to become uncluttered so that you could be open to suggestions.

Coping With Changes

Changes are going to happen in your life whether it is leaving your familiar surroundings, starting or ending relationships, or making career choices. Some people will find changes a welcome distraction and an opportunity at new beginnings. Others may find themselves immobilized in fear and doused in anxiety at the thought of making changes. The circumstances that necessitate the changes may be what is needed to prove that you are worthy of far more than you give yourself credit for.

Are you someone who makes lists with the pros and cons? A simple list of weighing up what's right, wrong, and what if turns into a thesis of why it should or should not happen. Raise your hands and jump up and down if you are one of those types of people? The very thought of making life-altering changes such as moving to another city, breaking up with your partner, or switching your major in college fills even the most serene person with fear.

Call on your celestial bodyguards to help you with your choices instead of relying on your lists. There is nothing wrong with asking for help. Those long lists may end up being redundant because the answers you seek are not as complicated as you first thought. The angels will give you the mental clarity you need to see through the fog, but you have to be open to their suggestions. Not everything can be handed to you on a silver platter and you may have the option to explore other avenues you never considered.

Financial Assistance

The angels are not going to come and shower you with dollar bills. The spheres don't have ATMs, nor are there any banks with billions of dollars or any other currencies. So, if you were getting excited at the thought of asking your angels to drop some bills for that pair of Nike Jordans you wanted—sorry to disappoint you.

Stress and concerns regarding finances are something everyone is worried about. People are struggling to keep their heads above the water to make ends meet. I want to reassure you that you are not the first—and you won't be the last—to find yourself in this position. We are not going to point and wag fingers at the economists or world leaders because that will be a never-ending game of blame.

Call on your angels for help and guidance. Look out for signs that will help guide you in the right direction. Practice patience and trust that your call for help has been received. You need to believe that help will come, even if it is just a positive attitude to gently shove you in the right direction. I cannot stress enough that you need to have an open mind at all times. Be open to receiving messages of help and guidance. This is where God teaches us that time and space in heaven work differently than they do on earth. What seems like a lifetime to us is only seconds for Him. If you don't want to believe that God is in control, then believe and trust that your request will be addressed at a time that is convenient to the universe.

Other Examples

Still not convinced that calling on angels for help is something worth your while? Firstly, it won't cost you a single dime. Secondly, you don't have to entertain them. Thirdly, you don't have to feed or hydrate them. All they want is for you to call on them for help, to trust them, to believe in them, and to be appreciative.

Okay, so you don't need help finding something, you don't need financial assistance, and you don't need help making life-altering choices or changes. Guess what? Those were examples of what people most often ask for. Come on, open your heart, and trust that something good will happen in your world. Let's take a look at a list of your angel calling cards.

- arriving at your travel destination safely
- daily protection for your loved ones

- mental stability and clarity when taking tests or giving a speech
- calmness during times of stress and depression
- mental affirmations to encourage weight loss and health
- a bubble to protect you from all negativity
- placing a filter in front of your mouth to prevent harmful words from being expelled
- deferring pain in your body to help you complete tasks
- energy to clean your home, work in the garden, or do the laundry

The list is endless as to what you can ask for. Hey, you don't have anything to lose by relying on a little bit of angelic and spiritual assistance. I do believe that I will make a believer out of you by the time we reach the end of this book.

How to Activate Angel Calling Cards

You know how to look out for signs that the angels are trying to communicate with you. You also know that you can ask the angels for just about anything under the sun. The final section of this chapter is going to show you how you can reach out to the angels. You have a choice of communication channels to reach out to the angels which do not include telephonic or digital means. Don't be afraid to be creative when activating the angel calling cards. The requests will be received and the appropriate messengers will be dispatched to offer support, guidance, protection, or whatever you need.

Writing

Not everyone likes to bare their souls and speak about what is going on in their lives. Holding onto unspoken emotions can cause more harm than good to one's soul. Everyone needs an outlet to get rid of whatever is holding them back. I am an advocate of journaling. Writing about your thoughts, feelings, and intentions is an excellent way to let your angels know that you need their help. You can always write letters, seal them in envelopes, and burn them in the fireplace so that no one else can see what you have asked or said to the angels.

Performing Arts

I believe that angels love to sing, dance, and play musical instruments because it allows them to re-energize their batteries. The angels work tirelessly to get messages to us or are busy guiding us so that we don't wander down the wrong path. The least we can do for them is indulge them in creative ways by singing, dancing, or playing the guitar. Show the angels what you would like by performing for them.

Verbal Communication

Have you ever caught yourself talking to someone that was not in the room with you? I'm not referring to having someone on speakerphone or ranting about someone who is not there to defend themselves. Would it be possible, maybe just a hint of possibility, that you were speaking to an angel and you didn't realize it? It wouldn't be such a far-fetched idea if you were talking to someone you couldn't see. The chances are that your angel is right there beside you, anxiously waiting for you to say the magic word or utter the code for help. I know for a fact that when I am talking to thin air, I do like to think I'm having a conversation with the angels.

Meditation

I embrace the quiet times when I am either meditating or praying. This is part of my daily ritual. I enter a world where all is calm and no one is rushing me to finish this or to make rash decisions when I am in prayer. It is the best part of my day, and normally happens before I go to sleep. However, lately, I have been parking my butt in my meditation chamber when I am frustrated or someone has done something I didn't like. I close my eyes and envision that I am calling for help to calm me down and I beg for help so that I won't lose my unsaved work while the laptop is having a nervous breakdown. There may or may not be a couple of cries for help but that all depends on the day and the situation.

My nighttime meditation ritual is slightly different. At night I immerse myself in the word and I pray to God my Father. On nights when I am feeling restless and I hear the rest of the neighborhood's dogs barking, I ask God directly for help: "Father God, may I ask for some angels to stand guard on all four corners of the property? May they protect any evil from entering the property? May they keep us safe? It would be greatly appreciated if it is your will, Father. This home and this property is yours Father, where your word is gospel." It is during these prayers that I visualize the angels with their trumpets and flames descending upon my house to protect us and keep us safe.

In Conclusion

Let down your guard, open your mind, and be welcoming of the angels that are swirling around you. Find a way to call them or involve them in your life that fits with your personality and attitude. Always remember that my methods may work extremely well for me, but they may not work for you. It is not a competition to see who can get their angel calling cards answered or activated the fastest. Some may need a little more work than others but patience and not giving up is the name of the game.

It is time to move on to the Angel Guide. You have an understanding and knowledge now of what the angel realm looks like. You know how to spot the signs of when an angel is in your presence. You know what you can ask for—which is pretty much whatever you want. And, you know how you can reach out for help, guidance, love, and/or protection.

The Angel Guide

Introduction to the Angel Guide

I had you running around the dusty archives as you explored the celestial hierarchy, spinning around in circles, and learning how to identify messages from angels—including why and how you could ask for assistance or guidance. I wanted to give you a guide that would be easy to understand and follow, but also be informative to build up your knowledge reserves.

I have previously indicated that believing and/or communicating with angels is a personal choice for everyone. You don't need a special prayer or ritual to call on angels for help. You don't have to be religious or belong to a specific religion to believe that angels are around us. Be who you have always been, because I have realized that you can't please everyone. It is time for everyone to give their fellow human beings a piece of the ground they walk on, a ray of sunshine, and a bit of blue sky or clouds. The world was not created for one person to be superior and selfish; it was created for millions and billions of people and animals to live together in peace and harmony.

The Angel Guide that I have created is going to be useful to every single person. It doesn't matter whether you are a Christian, Jew, Muslim, a member of The Church of Jesus Christ of Latter-day Saints, Catholic, a Pagan, or an atheist. All that matters is that you are here and a part of the rat race we call life. Bring your curiosity and questions about what is going on in the space around you and, hopefully, we can all learn and understand why certain things keep happening in our lives. This is a one-size-fits-all type of book where everyone is free to make decisions that are right for them. This is a bully-, judgment-, and discrimination-free journey that is between you and the angels accompanying you.

Are you ready to explore the Angel Guide? Yes, I am!

Are you ready to get to know your angels personally? Yes, I am!

Are you ready to meet the archangels, angels, and fallen angels? Yes, I am!

Are you sure that you are ready to meet everyone? Yes! I! Am!

Okay then, let's get going…

Archangels

You were introduced to archangels in Chapter 1 and where they rank on the celestial ladder. They may find themselves in the third sphere, which is furthest from God who is in the first sphere, but it doesn't make them any less important in the heavenly realm. As we previously learned, the meaning of archangel means "Chief Angel," which means that they are considered to be very powerful and have special abilities.

Archangels are appointed by God to tend to different areas of our lives that need attention, direction, or any type of help.

It is not certain how many archangels are at our beck and call because the Bible doesn't refer to many angels by their names. As it is, only three of the archangels are mentioned in the Bible and some of the others are referred to by the areas of their expertise. We know that there are many different religions and each has its own beliefs. I love the idea of having more angels who add purpose to my life. It is crazy to imagine only having a certain number of chief angels to help over 6 billion people.

I know of people who are too afraid to call on angels for help or to ask God for help because they don't want to be an unnecessary burden. We need to understand that these chief angels are only too happy to be needed because they are selfless entities who were handpicked by God to help us. They want to help us and they want to please God.

It is time now to meet the archangels. Together, we will be introduced to them and see what their divine responsibilities are. Who knows, I may have met one of these chief angels during my journey through the maze of life and didn't even realize it.

Archangel Michael

The Hebrew translation of the name Michael means "who is like God," or "gift from God." Archangel Michael is also known as the Warrior Angel because of his role as protector over heaven and earth. This "Chief Angel" was appointed by God to lead the angels. He is the only angel in the Bible to be identified by his name and rank of archangel Michael. Another interesting piece of information is that archangel Michael only utters four words throughout the whole Bible, and these can be found in Jude 9. It is a scene where the devil is arguing with archangel Michael about Moses' body, but instead of falling prey to the trap the devil is trying to set, he says: "The Lord rebuke you!"

We have people who believe that archangel Michael guards Israel and its people to ensure that they are protected. The responsibilities of this powerful, no-nonsense archangel don't end as the guardian of Israel, the protector of heaven and earth, or the leader of all angels. Oh no, archangel Michael is a very busy angel and has a list that doesn't begin to scratch the surface of what he does.

If you were to look at artwork depicting what the artist believes archangel Michael would look like, you would likely see him wielding a sword. Seeing the image of him with the sword is reaffirming that he is our protector and that we can call on him for protection when we experience periods of fear, confusion, or concern for our well-being. Calling on archangel Michael to protect our homes during times of conflict will cover your troubled and weary heart with peace and calm, and he blankets you in pockets of pillowy protection.

Archangel Michael has a lot more protection left in him if you were to call on help. If he can't help, he will know who to direct your cry for help to. Let's take a look at some of the help cries you may have:

- when you are stuck making difficult life decisions
- when you need an extra dose of courage to do something that scares you
- when you are stuck at a crossroads in your life and you need a nudge in the right direction
- when all the energy and zest for life has been drained from you because of negativity
- when you are lacking the motivation to make choices that will benefit your overall health and well-being
- when your self-worth is being challenged and you need a healthy "you are worth it" boost

Archangel Raphael

The Hebrew translation of Raphael means "healing of the Lord," or "God heals." It would be fitting for archangel Raphael to be referred to as the angel of healing. Archangel Raphael may not be mentioned in the Bible, but he does join the angelic lineup as an esteemed and powerful archangel. When archangel Michael fell to earth while battling with the devil, archangel Raphael was a heaven-bound angel who didn't have a human body.

Archangel Raphael's healing nature emphasizes his peaceful demeanor. He wants us to forgive those who hurt us, as well as be accountable for our actions against others. God didn't appoint archangel Raphael to be the angel of healing who dishes out all the gifts when asked. We have to be prepared to show respect and remorse for any wrongdoing against us. I have been hurt so many times that my anger meter has broken a couple of times, but then I feel a calmness come over me that lets me know that I should forgive these people because they don't know what they are doing.

I spoke to someone who suffers from extreme anxiety disorder who was willing to share their testimony with me. Anxiety affects people in many different ways, but for this person, their anxiety was triggered at night when they are falling asleep or when the telephone rings. They say that they can almost feel a hand stroking their hair and with each stroke, the anxiety slowly fades when they are falling asleep at night. When speaking to someone on the telephone, while sobbing and gasping for air, the caller will pause and change the conversation to something else to give them a moment to calm down. I honestly believe that archangel Raphael brings with him peace and tranquility while healing those who need his assistance.

Archangel Raphael is one of the leading archangels and he was tasked with helping people who struggle with an array of physical, mental, and spiritual ailments. The list of duties doesn't stop with assisting people who have ailments, it also includes people who provide healing and assistance such as medical professionals, spiritual guides, ministers, or pastors. Archangel Raphael's resume includes that he is also the patron saint of travelers that ensures that everyone gets to their destinations safely. We have archangels Raphael and Michael joining forces to help you feel the healing and comfort during times of fear or extreme stress that may impact your life negatively. You can call on archangel Raphael to be your guide with any health-related concerns you may have. Let's take a look at what type of calls of help you may have for archangel Raphael:

- you or someone close to you has been diagnosed with an illness or disease
- you have suffered a physical injury
- you struggle with depression or anxiety
- you struggle with substance abuse or addictions such as drugs, alcohol, or smoking
- you are struggling with your beliefs

- you are feeling alone and worthless
- you are angry and/or blaming God or the universe for what is happening in your life

Archangel Gabriel

The Hebrew translation of Gabriel means "God is my strength," "God is my strong man," or "hero of God." Archangel Gabriel is one of two good angels to be mentioned, by name (without his rank), in the Bible. He is referred to in scripture a total of four times. Daniel 8:15–26 sees Gabriel appear to Daniel after a disturbing vision where a shaggy goat and a two-horned ram are fighting. Gabriel appears in the form of a man who interprets the vision of an event that will take place between Greece (goat) and Persia (ram) in the distant future. The second time archangel Gabriel appears is in Daniel 9:21–27 in answer to Daniel's prayers of confusion regarding the vision about the goat and ram. God sends archangel Gabriel to clear up the confusion and gives him a clearer understanding of what the vision will entail when it becomes a reality.

Gabriel appears to Zechariah in Luke 1:19–20, where he introduces himself and explains that he was sent by God to share the good news and prepare him for the birth of Jesus Christ to be born from a virgin mother. Luke 1:26–38 sees Gabriel appear to Mary to prepare her for the news that she was chosen as the highly favored one to give life to Jesus. Gabriel leaves Mary as she professes: "'I am the Lord's servant,'

Mary answered. 'May your word to me be fulfilled.' Then the angel left her."

It is no wonder that archangel Gabriel would be referred to as the Messenger Angel. People are not satisfied with what they read and have to analyze and scrutinize words and information to paint a picture of the person of interest. Yes, people have concluded that archangel Gabriel is a scary-looking man based on the scripture as referred to in the previous paragraphs. I don't believe in judging a person, whether it is a human being or a member of the spiritual realm, on their appearance. I am content as long as their hearts and intentions are pure.

We know that archangel Gabriel acts as God's messenger and that he responds to our prayers. We have also come to learn that archangels like to stretch themselves thin to cover all the bases of what we may need. Let's take a look at some more of the duties on archangel Gabriel's list and why we may need his expert help in our lives:

- You may need inspiration when starting a new project or job.
- You may need energy that doesn't come in a liquid or solid form to help you with your ventures.
- You may want strength during difficult times.
- You may want a dose of determination to keep you focused on the task at hand.
- You may want to incorporate youthful playfulness to keep you from burning out.
- You may want help to achieve your goals without losing focus on your mental, physical, and spiritual health.

Archangel Jophiel

The Hebrew translation of Jophiel means "God's beauty." Angels are gender-neutral, meaning that they are neither male nor female, but the majority of archangels and angels are referred to by the male pronoun. I believe it would be safe to say that the angels can be whatever gender you want them to be. Artists have ideas of how they want to portray their subjects to the world. I do think that God and archangel Jophiel wouldn't mind if we imagined her to be a female because she is referred to as the Angel of Beauty.

Archangel Jophiel is not mentioned or referred to in the Bible, but she does form part of archangel Michael's army of warriors. She was hand-selected by God to watch over heaven and earth. Artists have depicted archangel Jophiel as holding a light. What do you think holding the light represents? I can think of a couple of examples which would include looking for a bright future, lighting the way for the lost, or filling our minds with light, bright, and beautiful thoughts.

Considering that archangel Jophiel represents all things beautiful, it would be fitting to add a little reminder here that you, the one reading this—yes, that would be you—are beautiful and handsome. No one cares about the zit that looks like a third eye in the center of your forehead or that wart under your eye. God created you in His image and in His eyes—you are perfect. Archangel Jophiel is not here to alter your looks. Let's take a look to see what we can call on archangel Jophiel to help us with:

- needing to see the beauty or light during storms when you don't see it yourself
- needing to change the negative thoughts that live in your head and be more positive
- to stop beating yourself up for not reaching certain achievements
- to see the beauty in everyone even though they are nasty people
- helping your creativity reach new and exciting levels
- help you to maintain calm and serenity in your life by slowing down to enjoy the beauty that surrounds you
- to shine her light of beauty and eliminate the negativity that threatens to darken our thoughts
- helping you to see your beauty the way God sees you

Archangel Ariel

The Hebrew translation of Ariel means "lion of God." Artists' imaginations have various visions of what archangel Ariel would look like if she were a human. We know that spiritual beings do not have bodies and when they appear to us in our dreams or visions, their appearances differ from person to person. The same applies to archangel Ariel, who has been depicted to be surrounded by the elements of nature such as earth, wind, fire, and water, including animals. It is no wonder that archangel Ariel would carry the title of the Angel of Nature and Animals.

Archangel Ariel is tasked with the protection of the plants and animals on the earth. She is also overseeing the care of the earth's elements namely: fire, wind, and water. We know that the elements of nature are and can be destructive to the environment. We have either witnessed the destruction for ourselves or we have seen media footage. I like to believe that these catastrophic events are meant to happen to prepare the earth for new growth. I don't believe God or archangel Ariel wants to see the earth being burned to a crisp or being washed away by water. I believe that they know stuff that we don't and that is why these events take place.

We know that archangel Ariel cares for and protects plants and animals. It would only be fitting that she works alongside archangel Raphael to protect and heal animals who have been hurt or are suffering trauma. Archangel Ariel will also oversee and help heal the earth that has been damaged. Non-religious people associate archangel Ariel as being a liaison officer between humans and mythical creatures such as fairies, sprites, or wood nymphs. May I just say that I love that we can all come together and allow our imaginations to run freely without the fear of being condemned for our different beliefs?

Let's take a look at some of the reasons why you would want to, or need to call on archangel Ariel for help:
- if your pet is not well
- if you see an injured animal
- you want to go hiking and need reassurance

- understanding and awareness related to the elements of nature
- fear of not having food, water, or a place to sleep
- protecting the environment from those who don't know how to show respect

Archangel Azrael

The Hebrew translation of Azrael is "whom God helps," "the help of God," or "helped by God." Artistic representation of archangel Azrael has him holding a bladed weapon which could be either a sword or a scathe, and he is clothed in a hooded garment. Many would say that this representation doesn't sound anything like the other archangels we have met until now. Others would be stomping around saying that you shouldn't be passing judgments based on your interpretation because what you see is not always what you get.

Archangel Azrael may be given the persona of the grim reaper wielding his bladed weapon and clocked in a hooded garment, but he is a gentle angel. As the Hebrew translation of his name would suggest, archangel Azrael helps God. How does he do this? He helps the souls of those who have passed away move on to the next realm. It would be only fitting to bestow the title of Angel of Death upon him.

Archangel Azrael is not solely responsible to help those who have passed away; he also helps their family members and friends by comforting them during the grieving process. As you may or may not be aware, grieving doesn't have a timestamp; and archangel Azrael will be around for as long as is necessary to heal the hearts and minds of those left behind. I do believe that archangel Azrael helps people from all walks of life and doesn't discriminate against anyone who does not follow alternative belief systems. It is also comforting to know that he would work with archangel Raphael to assist with the healing process. What would you need to call on archangel Azrael? Let's take a look at what his other avenues of expertise consist of:

- help and guidance when starting a new relationship
- help and guidance when a relationship ends
- help with substance abuse or additions
- help with understanding why a loved one had to pass away
- seeking affirmation that your loved one is at peace
- finding comfort after suffering a loss of a loved one
- help with strengthening your spiritual or religious beliefs
- help with moving forward in life instead of wallowing in heartache

Archangel Chamuel

The Hebrew translation of Chamuel is "one who seeks God," or "he who sees God." What do you think of when you see hearts and the mention of the color pink? Valentine's day? Love? Happiness? Peace? This is how artists have interpreted archangel Chamuel to look. Well, more like seeing him in some form of artistic creation that features him holding a heart or having one floating around him. Add in some peaceful color tones and you have an angel featuring a heart that is swaddled in pink colors. Should we be surprised that this archangel is named the Angel of Peaceful Relationships?

Archangel Chamuel may not have been mentioned in the Bible, but it is believed that he was referenced after Adam and Eve were kicked out of the Garden of Eden. He is also believed to have been referenced before Jesus was crucified. Archangel Chamuel was sent to comfort them and to bring peace to their souls. I love the idea of having someone (or an angel) give me comfort when I'm treading water and flooding my soul with peace and calm.

Archangel Chamuel is tasked with creating positive energy to drown out the negative. It is difficult, as human beings, to get rid of negativity—but thankfully powerful angels have the strength and patience to persevere until realization sets in. He is also a peace-loving archangel that wants to protect us and the world from strife and fear. Archangels Chamuel and Raphael work together when dealing with situations that involve pain, discomfort, anxiety, or depression. It is their job to work together to create peace and harmony while assisting with healing and restoring the imbalance. Let's take a look at some of the reasons why you may want to call on archangel Chamuel:

- to bring peace to communities who fight and make life impossible for those around them
- to fill you with peace and knowledge when setting out on a new career path
- to bring peace to a troubled soul that is cloaked in confusion
- to shine a light on new avenues to help you in your life's journey
- to mend broken relationships with family or friends

- to fill your heart with understanding before you leave your home each day
- patience with people who are known to rub you up the wrong way
- to forgive yourself for past wrongs
- to love yourself at all times

Archangel Chamuel concludes the lineup that makes up the seven most powerful archangels. You were introduced to the archangels and given a glimpse into the world they live in. I have mentioned previously that the exact number of archangels is not known to us. What is well-known to us is that two of the seven archangels, namely Michael and Gabriel, are referred to in the Bible. Michael is the only one identified and referred to by his rank of "archangel," while Gabriel is identified by his name as he appeared to Mary, Daniel, and Zechariah in their visions.

I want you to continue on this journey with me as we meet some more archangels. These angels are not as popular as the seven core archangels that we already know, but I felt it was important to include all archangels because we live in a diverse world and I love that everyone can be included. I want people to know that it is perfectly fine to have different religions and beliefs because no two people are alike. Can you imagine how boring the world would be if we were all the same? I can think of nothing worse than not being the person I was meant to be. I mean, after all, who would be writing books so that you can get to know your angels or understand what your angel numbers mean? No, we are happy being the individuals we are because we are better when we are not copying friends, family, or strangers.

Archangel Barachiel

The Hebrew translation of Barachiel is "God's blessings." It is no wonder that he is referred to as the Angel of Blessings. It is believed that archangel Barachiel delivers God's blessings to people who need a pick-me-up. Artists have portrayed archangel Barachiel to be wearing beautifully flowing white and pink robes, protectively holding a glowing white orb in his hands, as well as sporting his angelic white-feathered wings protruding from his back.

Archangel Barachiel brings joy and laughter as part of his blessings package. I have heard people talk about how they spontaneously start laughing when they are alone in a room or a car. Can you imagine how happy everyone on this earth would be if everyone started laughing without having a reason to? I do believe that laughter is medicine to the soul and that God would be soaking up every laughter because that is what He wants from us—to be happy. What are the reasons you would call on archangel Barachiel for?

- when you need a helping hand
- when you feel as if your life is worthless
- when you need a boost of confidence
- when you need to put the past where it belongs—in the past and start looking at the future
- when you are alone and feel as if no one cares
- when you need a good old belly laugh
- when you are looking for reassurance that you are where you need to be

Archangel Haniel

The Hebrew translation for Haniel means "grace of God." Archangel Haniel is known as the Angel of Joy because of her vibrant energy when she is in your presence. People have claimed to have been filled with hope and happiness after a period of hopelessness. The author of the book *The Angel Bible: The Definitive Guide to Angel Wisdom*, Hazel Raven, notes that archangel Haniel is bathed in shades of green. When you see these colors in your midst, you can be sure that you are receiving a visit from this outgoing archangel. Raven also mentions that archangel Haniel's colors include white which represents holiness, and light rays of green which represents healing and prosperity (Hopler, 2019a).

Is it any surprise why we would want to call on archangel Haniel to scoop us up out of our doomsday hole? One thing I have been hinting at throughout this book is that this world needs more joy and happiness. I totally understand that the world as we knew it was turned upside down. Many have started to reclaim their lives and move on from the devastation caused by a global pandemic that shows no signs of slowing down. It is time for every person to find good or happiness in themselves and their surroundings. I like to believe that when you start manifesting hope, joy, prosperity, or anything that triggers the happy genes in your DNA you will begin to notice smiles, hear laughter, and experience a sense of peace in the pit of your soul.

Archangel Haniel is waiting to spread her gorgeous wings and flutter in to help you realize your dreams. I would also wage a smile that archangel Haniel is waiting for you and me to call on her for help. Let's take a look at some examples of what she can help us with:

- guidance regarding spirituality or religion
- finding happiness in times when all hope seems lost
- understanding love and why it is important to you

Archangel Haniel wants you to be open to receiving her calling card. I understand that it is a tall order to open your heart and mind to love and receive any type of feelings relating to love. Throw all self-doubt out the window—don't sweep it under the rug where you can retrieve it again—and allow archangel Haniel to help and guide you to what you called on her for.

Archangel Israfel

The Islamic meaning of the name Israfel means "the burning one." Angels are not grouped according to religion. You don't need to feel intimidated when religion is referred to when being introduced to meeting these hardworking angels. I like to believe that angels are adaptable to whatever deity you believe in.

Archangel Israfel is believed to be the Angel of Music. Although he is not mentioned by name or rank in the Quran, he is believed to be one of the oldest archangels. His divine calling is to blow the trumpet to announce that the day of resurrection has arrived. He is believed to be standing on a holy rock in Jerusalem. Various spiritual leaders believe that archangels Raphael and Israfel are the same in their respective religious spheres.

Artistic representation of archangel Israfel believes he is tall and can reach the pillars of heaven from his spot in the celestial hierarchy. He has four wings with one protecting his body, one hiding him from God's line of vision, and one each pointing to the east and the west. Archangel Israfel is believed to have a beautiful voice and can serenade God in many different languages. Let's take a look at what we may call on archangel Israfel for:

- believing in the talent of singing and playing a musical instrument you were blessed with
- help with strengthening your vocal abilities
- reassurance that you have a beautiful voice that will touch the hearts of everyone hearing you
- reaffirming that your gift of music is part of your destiny

Archangel Jeremiel

The Hebrew translation of Jeremiel is "God uplifts." Jeremiel, when looking for a definition, means "mercy of God." Archangel Jeremiel is known as the Angel of Dreams for his ability to bring us messages when we are sleeping. It is true that most angels, when trying to send us messages or confirmation that they are with us, appear to us in our dreams. Artists have represented archangel Jeremiel appearing to us in our dreams as a vision swaddled in shades of purple.

Archangel Jeremiel is one of those angels who doesn't do much fanfare. One could almost assume that he is a made up member of the heavenly angels—you know, just to have names and titles to appease all people. I like to believe that he saves his energy so that he can fly in and out of our dreams to help us with our struggles. What could we call on archangel Jeremiel for:

- guidance about the path in which your life is going
- clarity that the decisions you are making are the right ones

- understanding errors in judgment and how to right what has been wronged
- help with problems that relate to your personal or professional life
- finding encouragement during the dark periods or when you find yourself stuck in your life maze and you cannot find the exit

Archangel Metatron

The definition of the name Metatron is "one who guards," or "one serves behind God's throne." Archangel Metatron is believed to be the Angel of Life. Some believe that he is the caretaker who ensures that no harm comes to the tree of life. He is also reported to notarize the good deeds of people who live on earth. The more archangels we meet, the more difficult it becomes to identify their names. Religion becomes skewed with everyone from all walks of life believing that they have different names for their angels. Archangel Metatron is no different and is referred to in various texts as being the angel of communication, as well as the patron saint of sick children.

I don't want us to get into a religious power struggle about who is right and who is wrong. We are all here to learn what we can through our interpretations and beliefs, and it is for that reason that I have decided to share all that I have learned about this powerful angel. Artists and visionaries have depicted archangel Metatron as having wings, clothed in violet and shining silver, and clutching a rotating cube in the palm of his hands. Others have the archangel Metatron guarding the tree of life. I can only imagine what it would be like to encounter this radiant archangel appearing in a cloud of violet and silver to help me with whatever I may need. Through my research and speaking to those who have encountered archangel Metatron, I am confident that he is someone we can call on for an assortment of issues and guidance we may need. Let's take a look at what we can call on archangel Metatron for:

- help in creating a healthy balance between work, extramural activities, and relationships
- help in taking control of the negativity and turning them into positive attributes
- help in breaking cycles of additions or unhealthy habits
- guidance on how to direct your spirituality for good
- guidance on clearing your mind of worry
- guidance on how to manifest miracles to make your life easier

Archangel Raguel

The Hebrew translation of Raguel is "friend of God." Artistic representation of archangel Raguel would have him wielding a gavel that resembles those used in the courts of justice. It is no surprise that archangel Raguel would be named the Angel of Justice and Harmony. The colors that accompany him are believed to be that of a pale blue or white which leads one to see his tranquil and peaceful side. Archangel Raguel is the peacemaker by ensuring that everyone between heaven and earth is happy and at peace.

I love to think that archangel Raguel is flitting between the different situations and touching all parties to let them know that we can all live together in peace and harmony. If everyone on this earth gave each other a little consideration, then we would all be walking around with smiles instead of frowns. I envision a happy world when I think about calling on archangel Raguel for assistance. I don't know about you, but I am tired of all the fighting about who is right or wrong, who was here first, or who is going to be around the longest. It is time for people to stop living in the past and future and start living in the present. Work together today to build a better tomorrow.

What else would we need to ask of archangel Raguel? Let's take a look and see what areas in our lives would benefit from calling in the help of a peacemaker:

- help in conquering an injustice that was done against you
- help in getting people to respect you as a person

- needing clarity about what to do when involved in a difficult relationship
- seeking guidance on how to deal with stressful situations
- seeking guidance on how to stand firm in your spiritual or religious beliefs when you feel as if you are under warfare
- help in finding peace and calm amid the chaotic life you find yourself in
- asking for help on behalf of loved ones or friends who need confirmation that they are not alone in this world and that they are worthy of love

Archangel Raguel, the peaceful angel clothed in the calming colors of pale blue and/or white, is waiting for you to call on him to help bring peace. He wants you to know that you can call on him regardless of the situation you find yourself in. Trust and believe that you will find peace, calm, and stability when you call on archangel Raguel.

Archangel Raziel

The Aramaic meaning of the name Raziel is "the Lord is my secret." It is no wonder that archangel Raziel would be known as the Angel of Mysteries. Artistic representations of archangel Raziel show him with his hands raised and holding a ring that resembles the infinity symbol while radiating a bright white light. Most archangels are defined by single colors, but archangel Raziel is rumored to appear sporting a rainbow of vibrant colors which shows his mysterious side.

Some believe that archangel Raziel's resume includes being the patron saint of law, as well as being tasked as the keeper of knowledge and wisdom. As human beings, we are curious. We believe it is our right to know everything—even things we don't have to concern ourselves with. We are not happy with the answers we are given and when we dig even further and deeper, we end up with more questions than answers. It is time for each one of us to realize and understand that we are not meant to know everything and that it is okay to have some secrets. All secrets will be revealed to us when the time is right.

What could we want archangel Raziel to help us with? Let's take a look and see if we can find a stash of secrets in our questions:

- a clear understanding of what to do when stranded at a spiritual crossroads
- a shove and a nudge from God or your deity to let you know that you are on the correct path
- help in reaching a larger audience when sharing useful insights and information
- help with searching for answers relating to the way the universe works and how you can benefit from the knowledge

- needing help and guidance to interpret dreams and find their true meaning

Archangel Sandalphon

The meaning of the name Sandalphon is "co-brother." It is believed that archangels Sandalphon and Metatron are brothers, or at the very least spiritual brothers. Some believe that archangel Sandalphon lived on earth as a human being, and others believe that he was once the prophet Elijah who was taken from the earth in a chariot of fire and light. Unfortunately, Scripture doesn't give us much information and it is purely speculation. I have to admit that I do enjoy the mystery around how the angels got their names and where they originated from. As previously mentioned, it is good to have an air of mystery to keep our imaginations active.

Artistic representation of archangel Sandalphon indicates that he is very tall and holding or playing a musical item. Another representation has archangel Sandalphon appear with beautiful wings protruding from his back, clothed in white robes, and carrying a golden harp that is glowing. It is no wonder that archangel Sandalphon is referred to as the Angel of Music, as well as recognized as the patron angel of music. It is believed that when he appears to people in their dreams or visions he comes in an illusion of pink and light green colors, and his beauty takes away the breath of those who see him. Archangel Sandalphon is not only the music maker but also acts as a messenger delivering prayers to whichever deity you are praying to and returning answered prayers.

I don't know about you, but I for one could do with more spiritual music to lighten the mood in my soul. Let's put my preferences aside and have a look at why you would want to call on archangel Sandalphon:

- you may need a good night's sleep
- you may need help finding your meditation groove
- you may want help relaxing
- you may want to ask for your prayer requests to be sent via speed mail

- you may want help with mastering your musical instrument of choice
- you may need help with your writer's block that is stunting your creativity
- you may want to ask for your soul to be calm and serene during times of extreme anxiety or worry

You have no limitations as to what you can ask archangel Sandalphon for. He is a powerful angel that exudes calm and healing energy. Don't be afraid to ask him for help—he will take your prayers to where they need to be and have them answered in the best manner possible for your circumstances. I do want to remind you again that you can ask for whatever you want, but you have to be open-minded to believe that you will get an answer. You should not ask for help, wait a day, and give up hope. Time works differently in the spiritual realm than how it works on earth. Practice patience and have hope.

Archangel Uriel

The Hebrew translation of Uriel is "angel of light," "flame/fire of God," or "God is my light." Artists have varying representations of what archangel Uriel looks like. One representation would have him dressed in white with his wings protruding from his back and carrying what would be described as a lantern. Another representation would show archangel Uriel with an open book in his hands. One more representation has archangel Uriel carrying a torch or what may look like the sun in his hand. These representations seem to be fitting considering the translation of his name.

Archangel Uriel, unfortunately, does not carry the name of the angel of light as his name would suggest. Instead, he has been given the name of the Angel of Wisdom. It is believed that the light that he carries is a beacon for people who need help making difficult decisions. I like the idea of archangel Uriel standing, like a lighthouse, calling struggling individuals and letting them know that he is ready to help them find direction in their lives. Let's take a look at some of the reasons why you may find it necessary to call on archangel Uriel:

- looking for help to break the destruction caused by mental health issues
- asking for guidance when considering a new career
- opening your heart and mind to be accepting of God's answer when requesting prayer for specific needs
- being open to accepting and learning information that is outside of your comfort zone

- asking for comfort during times of loneliness

When asking archangel Uriel for help or guidance, you have to be open to receiving messages in unconventional ways. We have learned that angels are cloaked in a cloud of mystery and they want us to work for our messages. It is also a way for them to test your faith in them. So, when you are expecting help from archangel Uriel, start looking out for visions or dreams, written messages in the form of poetry or quotes, or when you are meditating after a tough day at the office.

I would like to insert a disclaimer here and remind you that angels are not medical professionals. You are asking for guidance and direction in your life. I don't believe it is fair to ask the angels questions about medication. Angels are here to guide us and help us, not to give us advice. Regardless of where you are on your spiritual or religious journey, you need to consult your doctor before discontinuing or altering your medication. Don't ever do something that goes against what medical professionals tell you to do.

Archangel Zadkiel

The meaning of the name Zadkiel has various definitions which include "God is my righteousness," "God is my kindness," "grace of God," and "angel of mercy." Artistic representation of archangel Zadkiel has him wielding a bladed weapon resembling a knife. Members of the Jewish faith believe that archangel Zadkiel is the one who appeared to Abraham and stopped him from sacrificing his son, Isaac, in Genesis 22. If the representation is accurate, it would make sense that he would be called the Angel of Mercy. Along with his title of being the angel of mercy, it is believed that archangel Zadkiel is the patron angel of forgiveness among people.

Carrying around unresolved anger, hatred, and guilt each day cannot be healthy for anyone. Can you imagine how Abraham must have felt when God told him to sacrifice Isaac? He must have had many emotions, but he suppressed them all because he loved God so much that he would do anything to make Him happy. How would you react if the tables were turned and you were put in that position? Your faith, belief, and spirituality are put to the test every day. Everything you do is tested to see how you will react in any given situation. I do believe that this is why archangel Zadkiel is the angel of mercy, as well as the patron angel of forgiveness.

I know that it may seem intimidating to picture archangel Zadkiel wielding a bladed weapon, but let's have a little faith in this angel of mercy. Let's take a look at what you may call on archangel Zadkiel for:

- need help to break the cycle of negative feelings and emotions
- forgiveness against those you may believe wronged you
- needing healing from situations where abuse has caused you to be wary of everyone
- seeking forgiveness from God or your deity for intentionally causing harm to others
- needing help and guidance to cope with mental and physical pain caused by others
- looking for help to heal broken friendships or relationships

In Summary

This concludes the meet and greet of your archangels. It is wonderful to learn that all the archangels play an important part in our lives. I have found it incredibly inspiring that all the archangels work together to ensure that we have someone watching over us. I will admit that I found it slightly cheeky to have such powerful angels hiding out in the last sphere of the celestial hierarchy. It wasn't until I got to know the archangels that I changed my way of thinking and selfishly agreed that they are needed where they are.

Each of the archangels was given a title. They were entrusted by God, Allah, Muhammad—or whoever you believe in—to be your and my protector. We get to call on the archangels to help us with whatever we need, and our requests are directed to who is best suited to deal with our circumstances. What about the people who don't believe? It's your choice to believe or not. I have mentioned multiple times since you started reading this book that I am not going to force or coerce you into believing anything. You do have a choice and no one, not even me, can take that away from you. All that I did ask of you was that you have an open mind when reading through this book.

What have you learned during your meet and greet with the archangels? Have you learned anything new that you didn't know before? Have you become more aware of your surroundings? I would like to share a list of what I have learned about archangels.

- I have learned that the archangels work together to bring healing and comfort or healing and understanding.
- I have learned that archangels are not as scary as art or text would suggest.
- I have learned that archangels have my best interests at heart.
- I have learned that archangels don't do anything without being told by God or other deities.
- I have learned that the archangels are patiently waiting for me to reach out to them for help, guidance, compassion, or love.
- I have learned that I need to have an open mind and be accepting of the messages or signs they leave for me.
- I have learned that when I am praying, God hears me and 'patches' me through to the right archangel department.
- I have learned that I have a greater understanding of the roles that archangels play in our everyday lives that affect us either directly or indirectly.

Let's give the archangels a moment to enjoy some fresh air while they flit around to keep an eye on the rest of the world. It is time to move on to the second section of this Angel Guide. Let's get going!

Angels

The time has come for me to introduce you to the angels that find themselves in the third sphere of the celestial ladder. Angels (or guardian angels) find themselves to be the furthest from the very top of the spheres where God sits and has a clear view of the whole world. At the beginning of Chapter 1, I pointed out that no matter where you find yourself in life—whether you are working for a multi-billion-dollar corporation or bagging groceries at Target—the position you hold, regardless of how significant or insignificant it may seem to you, is important. You were chosen for your position for a reason and the chances are that if you are bagging groceries, you will be noticed by people as you greet them with a smile. All it takes is a smile or a friendly greeting to let people know that you see them.

You were introduced to 17 archangels in the previous section of the Angel Guide. The first seven you were introduced to are believed to have been hand-picked by God. Archangel Michael is the commander of all the angels throughout the three spheres, but he sits in the third sphere. He is the one that gets his orders from God and hands out assignments to all the angels. I believe that archangel Michael deals with a lot of angry humans, but let us not forget that he is the one who assisted when it came to ousting the devil from heaven. Yes, archangel Michael fell from heaven during the struggle—but he was rewarded for his bravery.

No one can say how many angels reside in heaven. I do believe that different beliefs and religions play a part in who the angels are and what their roles are in our lives. I would like you to visualize an image in your mind as you read this. Picture the archangels standing side by side as they line a couple of football fields. Now envision that each archangel has a row of angels lining up in front of them. Now you are watching as the archangels leave the front of the row and stop at each angel to hand them a scroll. The angels open the scrolls to see their daily list of chores. The list of chores are the names of people who have requested help or guidance for any number of areas of concern.

The archangels reach the end of their respective rows after all the scrolls have been handed out. They spread their wings and push up off the ground as they rise above the angels. The angels only have eyes for their archangel as they are given a blessing to go out and do good.

The vision I have shared is one that I have had in my mind's eye before I ever thought about writing this book. Some may say it was a childhood dream that was created and others may say that I had an overactive imagination; I like to believe that I find solutions when nothing else makes sense. Please remember to send up a massive "thank you" if and when you are blessed by an angel.

I do believe that we have reached the part of this Angel Guide where we get to meet some of the angels that may have crossed our paths. I am hoping that when I introduce you to the angels that you may have an "aha" moment when you realize that you have been sun-kissed or feather-touched by an angel.

Meeting Your Angels

The list of angels is long, and I had to decide who I believed needed to be mentioned. I don't, for one moment, want you to think that if the angel that you may have encountered is not listed, that they are not significant. I want you to know that the names of angels differ from person to person. Some people may prefer to identify their angels with the names of their loved ones or pets that have passed on. It is all a matter of personal preference.

Angel Achaiah

Angel Achaiah is the guardian angel for individuals born between April 21 to April 25. Her duties as an angel do not end there. Angel Achaiah is also referred to as the Angel of Patience. She has an impressive resume that includes protecting individuals from lies and negativity, and filling people with infinite wisdom and humility to bring out the best abilities of themselves. Angel Achaiah gives us an insight into people we meet that goes past their appearances. People are quick to look at what a person looks like and pass judgment based on their preferences without looking at their minds and hearts. I love that there is an angel that can give me an x-ray view that penetrates deeper than the surface.

Call on angel Achaiah when:
- you need an extra dose of patience
- you need more perseverance to achieve the results of the task you set out to do
- you need a confidence boost to remind you that you have done the best you could do
- you need positivity that you will get the job you wanted but if you don't, to understand that it wasn't meant to be
- you would like your mind to be freed from all the cobwebs that have been holding you back on the path to success

Angel Aladiah

The name Aladiah means "God's promising or encouraging," or "favorable God." It is no wonder that she would be referred to as understanding, forgiving, and filled with grace. Angel Aladiah's followers are believed to be more aware of their mistakes or errors in judgment when going about their daily tasks. She symbolizes everything that is fair and just by figuring out their mistakes without folding under the pressure. This angel wants to protect those who call on her for help or guidance. She instills a sense of peace which makes it easier for you to forgive someone who has hurt you in any way. Angel

Aladiah's list does not end there—she has proven that she is worth her weight in gold because she just wants to envelop everyone with all things positive. I do believe that we all need a protector like angel Aladiah, so make sure you call on her when:

- you need to practice patience at work or home when dealing with a difficult situation
- you need a clear head when making possible life-altering decisions
- you need help recognizing mistakes and failures, and preventing them from reoccurring in the future
- you need to remember that you have morals that were instilled in you by your caregivers and that you need to remember where you came from
- you need people to stop throwing your past wrongdoings in your face when you have proven time and again that you are not the same person you once were

Angel Amatiel

Angel Amatiel is known as the Angel of Hope. It would be fitting to give her the title of the beacon of life and new beginnings. As humans, we are set in our ways and we are afraid to have hope or believe in something because, sad as it may seem, we are wired to believe that everything comes at a price. We are going to change our way of thinking and look at the way the world turns by believing in angel Amatiel and having hope. What do you have to lose? You only have one life, and you need to live life to the fullest. Fill your buckets with hope, belief, and an abundance of joy. Please join me in making the future better and brighter for ourselves, including our friends, family, and everyone surrounding us.

Call on angel Amatiel when:

- you need encouragement when things are not going according to plan
- you need help overcoming struggles.

- you are ready to make changes in your life that will bring about positivity
- you are ready to accept that it's okay to fail and that it isn't a weakness
- the river that flows with hope and rebirth will fill you up and drown you in all things bright and beautiful

Angel Amitiel

Angel Amitiel is referred to as the Angel of Truth and Understanding. This spritely angel is believed to love all people regardless of their circumstances, sins, gender, ethnicity, or career. She gives her love freely to all who may want it, whether they need it or not. You will feel angel Amitiel's presence surrounding you when you are being true to yourself and those around you. I believe that we have to love and respect ourselves before we can touch the lives of others. Angel Amitiel wants you to take stock of what is happening in your mind, body, and soul—and this will help you understand your emotions. You will begin to feel the love and experience emotions you never knew possible once you have opened the window to let in the light.

Call on angel Amitiel when:
- you are ready to allow the light into your heart
- you need help and guidance through difficult transitions that affect your relationship with people
- you need help to become a better person with greater values that include compassion for your fellow humans
- you are struggling to understand why your new attempts at change are not working the way you envisioned
- you need to feel love and happiness after experiencing a period where nothing has gone the way you had envisioned

Angel Anachel

Anachel means "grace of God," or "angel of grace." This graceful angel is believed to appear to you by holding her heart in the palm of her hand. The intention is so that you can absorb the love she so freely wants to bless you with. Every single person walking around on this earth has a purpose, and until you start investigating yourself and taking stock of your life, you won't know what you are destined for. I bet you have been told multiple times by doting parents and family members that you have a destiny to fulfill. I was one of those individuals who was constantly reminded about purpose and destiny. I honestly didn't know what everyone was talking about until I started writing. Knowing that my words may be what you or your neighbor might need to hear has ignited a fire within me. In short, God's plan for me hasn't failed me yet and I know that I still have many miles left on the odometer before I can declare that my destiny or purpose has been fulfilled.

Call on Angel Ananchel when:

- you need confirmation that you are on the right path during your journey through life
- you feel that the love in your soul is not adequate to do the task that is needed
- you want to sing your praises of thanks for the blessings of grace that have been poured into your heart
- you start feeling as if you are abusing your gift from God by being selfish or for selfish gain
- you feel that you aren't being rewarded with the gift of grace or you need a reminder that you need to give gifts to receive gifts

Angel Anauel

Angel Anauel symbolizes courage and supporting causes that improve one's standing in the community. It is believed that this angel's name means "infinitely good God." Angel Anauel graces those who follow him with superb health and tries to assist (when asked) for financial security. It is said that people who call on him for help and guidance will become rich without compromising their integrity. I learned something from my research about angel Anauel that I found interesting—and that was that if you believe in him, you will avoid illness. One thing I have learned is that if you are protected by angel Anauel you have an outgoing personality and you will rake up friends, persons of interest, or possibly even future business associates. I do believe that anyone who is lucky enough to call on angel Anauel for assistance will be abundantly blessed and fortunate to have such an empowering angel guiding them through any situation because of their ability to be strong and courageous, yet authoritative and grounded.

Call on Angel Anauel when:

- you need a boost in your financial standing that is not for selfish purposes such as buying a Bugatti La Voiture Noire or booking a trip to Mars
- you need help negotiating with difficult customers to grow your business in a way that benefits many people
- you need help to repair or build stronger relationships with friends, family, or colleagues
- you feel that your health is taking a dive in the wrong direction, so you want to heal faster so that you can carry on working or focusing on building healthy business relationships
- you need to see that there is a light at the end of the tunnel and that all you are doing—both in your business, career, or personal life—is not in vain

Angel Aniel

Aniel means "God of virtues," and it is no wonder why he would be referred to as the Angel of Courage and Virtue. Angel Aniel encourages you to be strong and determined in life so that you don't fall prey to any weakness that wants to break down your foundations. This mighty angel wants to help you normalize your emotions and build you up. Angels want to help and guide you to bring out the best of you so that you can spread your gifts with people you come in contact with. It is no secret that humans are creatures of habit, and we are not the most patient when looking or asking for guidance or assistance in various areas of our lives. Angel Aniel is standing by, ready with his basket of tricks and tools, to help you grow stronger, enrich your creativity, and give you the courage you need to stand up and claim your life.

Call on angel Aniel when:

- you feel as if no one is listening to you and they are talking down to you or dismissing your ideas
- you want a little nudge to perfect your ambition to be more selfless to include people who don't have the happiness, love, or creativity that you have received
- you need a little help readjusting to new rules or routines
- you need help to deal with challenges in your life without losing focus on what is important
- you want more balance or positive energy when you have reached a point in your life where you feel that nothing is working for you

Angel Asaliah

The meaning of the name Asaliah is "just God who tells the truth," and it is believed that angel Asaliah is a male angel. As you already know, the gender of angels—and who and what we believe them to be—should not make a difference to us. Angel Asaliah is a thinker who looks at a situation or circumstance before taking action. He is known as the Angel of Intellect and Memory, and it is no wonder that he wants the people who call on him to reflect on their actions. I believe that you need to reflect on what you have done and then rectify the situation. That way, you will have a clear conscience and you may just learn a couple of truths you have ignored about yourself.

Call on Angel Asaliah when:

- you need peace of mind when entering a meeting which may determine your future

- you need help with understanding a difficult problem without affecting your mental clarity by overthinking the solution
- you need a nudge to remain truthful to friends, family, and peers at all times, regardless of how difficult it may be

Angel Cassiel

The meaning of the name Cassiel is "speed of God." Angel Cassiel is believed to be part of the seven heavenly archangels, but research leads us to believe that he was human before becoming an angel. Angel Cassiel is rumored to be a lonely angel who is also known as the Angel of Tears. He has also been tasked with being the guardian of planet Saturn. I like to think that angel Cassiel sits on his revolving ring as he keeps a close eye on what is happening on earth and reports his findings to the archangels. Tarot cards have depicted angel Cassiel to be wearing black and wielding a scythe leading people to believe that he is the angel of death. Of course, you know this is not true because you have been introduced to the archangel Azrael who is the angel of death. You are most probably wondering what type of help or guidance you could possibly need from this poor and lonely angel of tears.

Angel Cassiel cannot interfere with the choices you make and he can't nudge you to make a decision, but he can surround you with his presence to let you know that you are never alone. He can also be your support angel who will guide you to make the right decisions without affecting your choices. I have a sneaky suspicion that angel Cassiel may just be the voice that lets you know you are barking up the wrong tree when you believe you are making the right decision. Let's take a look at why you may need to call on angel Cassiel:

- you find yourself in a difficult situation such as being laid off at work, someone you love has been diagnosed with an incurable disease, or a loved one has passed away unexpectedly
- you are alone and not feeling included in what's going on around you even though you are surrounded by people who care

- you suspect that someone you care about is not in the best spiritual position of their life and you ask for help in guiding their soul

Angel Cahetel

The meaning of the name Cahetel is "God of blessings." It is believed that angel Cahetel possesses an abundance of luck, righteousness, and wisdom. He is also known as the Angel of Reality because of his ability to keep you grounded and educate you to be happy with what you have. I love the idea of being taught to be content with just enough and not to be greedy and want everything so that no one else can benefit. Angel Cahetel attempts to ward off bad spirits or negative entities from entering your life. He will guide you to find your spiritual blessings that form part of your destiny. You may have been told by various friends and family that you should not give up on your dreams; Angel Cahetel is hovering around you and nodding his head in agreement. I am pretty sure that if you were to look around, you would find some feathers, because he is trying to get your attention to say that he agrees. Angel Cahetel wants to see your dreams become a reality. You can do whatever you put your mind to, and no one should ever squash your dreams or break your spirit. He wants you to be happy with your decisions and that is why he is going to be around you. Angel Cahetel wants to ensure that you believe in yourself, that you are happy with who and what you are, and that you are content with what you have without being greedy and taking more than you need.

Call on Angel Cahetel when:

- you need help with your work when you have reached a mental block and don't know how to change your way of thinking
- you need a spiritual realignment or cleansing to help you when you start feeling as if everything in your life is stacked against you and nothing is going according to the way you planned
- you want to express your gratitude to someone but you are struggling to make the words add up

- you need help expressing your thoughts or feelings when everyone around you seems to dismiss you

Angel Caliel

The name Caliel means "God ready to rescue." Angel Caliel is believed to be associated with the ranks of all things fair and honest. This sassy angel is a no-nonsense and fair-winged lady who is all about promoting innocence and honesty. Angel Caliel is the symbol of righteousness. She will bring her wings down on those who are guilty of injustice or wrongdoing. We know that angels are not vindictive in any way, shape, or form, and they will not hurt us. However, they will make your conscience work in such a way that you will have no other option but to confess and repair the damage you have caused. Angel Caliel wants to keep you on the straight and narrow, which is something everyone should adhere to.

Call on angel Caliel when:
- you need help with being honest with your work peers, friends, or family about choices that were made to promote yourself and failing your integrity
- you need help identifying when someone is taking advantage of a situation and letting them know they have been caught
- you want everyone to work together for the greater good instead of choosing sides because the grass may seem to be greener on the other side without weighing the pros and cons

Angel Chavaquiah

The name Chavaquiah means "God who gives joy." Angel Chavaquiah is believed to be the angel of reconciliation and harmony. She wants everyone to get along with each other to live in peace and harmony, as well as promote the strengthening of family bonds. Family doesn't necessarily have to be related by blood, they can also be people who are there for you when no one else is. Angel Chavaquiah can be seen as the voice of reason when people are not getting along with each other.

I find it extremely heartbreaking when families fall apart after the glue that binds them is no longer there. I heard about a lady who tried to be the glue after her mother passed away, but the younger sibling wouldn't have it. Instead, the younger sibling turned on the older sibling, brought up her past, and flung it in her face. The older sibling wasn't prepared to stoop to the younger sibling's level and list all the transgressions. The situation has reached a point where the older sibling struggles with anxiety and trust which are manageable, but the younger sibling is not moving forward in their life because of the tear they created in the family unity. Do I believe in karma? What you do to others will be done to you? Absolutely, and this is where I believe angel Chavaquiah enters the party. She doesn't like what she sees and puts a stop to any good happening to the younger sibling until they realize what they have done and repair the damage.

Call on angel Chavaquiah when:

- you need a referee to intervene during family brawls so that everyone understands where they are going wrong
- you want help in building a balanced and healthy relationship with people who are part of your life
- you want to make amends with someone who was hurt by a family member in the past

Angel Damabiah

The name Damabiah means "God fountain of wisdom." Angel Damabiah is recognized by her water-seeking symbol and it is, therefore, no surprise that she has been given the rank of Angel of Water. When looking at the meaning of her name, I only have to smile because I believe that God—or any other deities—only has to acknowledge that this would be regarded as the angel who allows all this good and positive flow from her fountain. Water is a very important feature for all life forms, ranging from humans and animals to plants, that need to thrive and survive. Angel Damabiah wants everyone to drink from the fountain so that they can build up their inner strength and succeed in wherever or whatever direction life takes them.

Angel Damabiah is the protector of all bodies of water. She uses the water to prevent negativity and hatred. It is part of angel Damabiah's heavenly duties to preserve and protect pure hearts, kind souls, and selflessness among all people. I like to imagine that after a busy day at work, I can relax in front of the television and feel the calming ebb and flow as angel Damabiah pulls the stress from my body and fills me with renewed energy.

Call on angel Damabiah when:

- you need confirmation that what you are doing or the path you are following is one that is going to be successful
- you need a gentle shove when you feel as if you have lost your way by becoming selfish or putting your needs above those of people who are more in need than you
- you need a boost of faith to remain hopeful that you will get the job that you applied for or that you will get that life-changing call from the doctor letting you know that you are healthy

Angel Daniel

The meaning of the name Daniel is "God is my judge." Daniel is a strong biblical name and should not be confused with the angel we are meeting. Angel Daniel's name is believed to be "the sign of mercies." I think it is safe to assume that we can refer to angel Daniel with the pronoun indicating his gender as being that of a male. Angel Daniel is believed to be an eloquent angel who does not allow anyone to push him around or shove him out of the way. He is the essence of honesty and when he is called upon for help, his followers will be forced to be truthful and honest in his presence. He will allow you to see the world with clarity and understanding when you are struggling to make difficult decisions or choices.

Call on angel Daniel when:

- you know that you have done something to intentionally harm someone else and your conscience needs a scrub down to help you deal with your mistakes and make amends
- you need help to strengthen the relationships you have with those who have always been your biggest supporters, but because of trust issues, you have forgotten how to weed out the true friends from the fake friends
- you are going through a difficult time after suffering the loss of someone close to you or you feel that you are in a bad situation and you need reassurance that your spiritual angel is comforting and guiding you

Angel Dokiel

Angel Dokiel is known as the "weighing angel," and it would make sense to give him the title of the Angel of Balance. It is believed that the angel Dokiel is described in the Testament of Abraham as being like the sun who balances it in the palm of his hand. It is further believed that he is tasked with keeping the balance between the planets and the cosmic world to work in perfect harmony. Furthermore, angel

Dokiel is believed to be one of two angels to examine the souls of the recently deceased before allowing them in through the pearly gates.

Angel Dokiel is responsible for keeping your life in balance. He will knock you down to size when you tilt a little too much to one side because it is his job to ensure that you remain true to yourself. Angel Dokiel's main task is to ensure that you experience a healthy balance when it comes to your mental, physical, emotional, and spiritual well-being. This is where you learn to trust in someone greater than you and believe that you need to bring a harmonious balance into your daily life. All too often we take on the problems of the world and we ingest way too many toxic words and acts because we don't know how to "drop and roll." Let's open our minds and hearts and allow angel Dokiel to restore the balance that has been disrupted.

Call on angel Dokiel when:

- you feel that you may need a spiritual realignment to create a healthy balance
- you need guidance with letting go of the emotional baggage that has been pulling you down
- you find yourself struggling with your physical health because you are too busy being concerned about everyone else around you that you neglect yourself
- you need to find balance in your life to do the things you love doing and do the things you need to do (we often forget to find a healthy balance between obligation and necessity)

Angel Elemiah

The meaning of the name Elemiah means "hidden God." Angel Elemiah is believed to be a bold, brave, and strong lady angel who is known to be the Angel of Success and Protection. The angel mediums have a soft spot for this protective angel who is not only curious and open-minded, but also exudes happiness, courage, strength, and success in everything she sets out to achieve. Those who call on angel Elemiah know exactly what they want from her and there is no doubt in their minds that she will make them work for what they need. This no-nonsense angel will not enable you, but she will help you by giving you nuggets of advice or sharing her pearls of wisdom with you along the way.

Angel Elemiah is tasked with ensuring that you are happy in the career you have chosen for yourself. She wants to fill you with the courage that is needed to move you out of your glass cage so that you can discover the world around you. Angel Elemiah wants to fill your mind with who, what, where, when, how, and why; and she also wants to activate the curious switch in your mind. You are letting angel Elemiah know that you are ready to be unleashed in the world so that you can explore your strength and bravery.

Call on angel Elemiah when:

- you are ready to make positive changes in your life
- you are ready to accept that you want your quality of life to improve, you need to make positive changes in the right direction
- you are ready to remove the shackles of your past life and hurt, and put the past where it belongs—in the past so that you can take a step forward without being pulled back

Angel Eyael

The meaning of the name Eyael means "delightful God of children and men." The angel mediums believe that he is the guardian angel of Pisces, the Zodiac sign. He is an understanding angel who visits those who call on him with an abundance of wisdom. Angel Eyael is one of those who promote positivity, which is what we should all be incorporating into our daily lives. He has a zest for life, and that is why he wants you to look for the silver lining around the darkest clouds before throwing your hands up in despair. Life has become one big giant bowl of Jell-O where we wobble, give up the fight because we jiggle a little too much, and wait to become a puddle of goo. It is time that we all find strength in our wobble, throw in an extra wobble with the jiggle (for good measure), and stand firm to prevent that puddle of goo from taking away your happiness. Angel Eyael wants us to stand together, help those that can't help themselves, and share our experiences with others.

It is believed that the people who call on angel Eyael have a passion for life, are adventurous, and are passionate about helping those in need. There is a very thin line between wanting to help everyone and being taken advantage of by people who expect, more than appreciate, what is being done. I do believe that angel Eyael is going to keep the balance to ensure all is fair. Angel Eyael comes across as very quiet and reserved, and I see this as a sign of his protective nature as he keeps a close eye on those who call on him. I can picture him with his wings wrapped around us and protecting us from all types of attacks such as misinformation being spread on social media, fear-mongering from conspiracy theorists, or hateful speech.

Call on angel Eyael when:

- you need a dose of positivity when you feel as if you are the only one in your circle who is thinking clearly and everyone else has slipped through the cracks
- you are struck with fear about making life changes and you believe when people tell you that you won't succeed
- you need a reminder that you don't have to be a hero and that it is okay to experience sadness or fear during times of uncertainty

Angel Muriel

The name Muriel means "perfume of God." I think it is fitting that angel Muriel's calling would relate to people's sense of smell. It is no wonder angel Muriel has been tasked with the duties of being the Angel of Intuition and Emotional Harmony. People who have encountered angel Muriel have described her to be wearing a crown made of the most beautifully scented flowers. They have also mentioned that they have seen her crown floating, ever so calmly, on the river of life. The next time you get a waft of your favorite flower, perfume, or food when you are either alone, not using any scent, or not cooking; I believe it is safe to assume that angel Muriel is popping in for a visit.

It is believed that angel Muriel is true to her title and helps anyone who calls on her by enveloping them with compassion and understanding when they are struggling with their emotions. Angel Muriel is also the protector of empaths. She can help those who struggle with the overwhelming emotions and feelings that they absorb from people around them. Angel Muriel can help empaths because of her ability to remain grounded.

Angel Muriel is believed to be part of the second sphere residents in the celestial hierarchy. She is believed to be part of the Dominion angels. As we learned in Chapter 1, Dominions don't have direct contact with God but they do get their messages and tasks via the first sphere angels. We also believed that Dominions don't interact with human beings. This leads me to believe that angel Muriel may be one of the angels in my vision that receives their tasks when standing in queues before the appropriate archangels.

Call on angel Muriel when:

- you need to restore peace and harmony in your life after a traumatic experience such as the death of a loved one or dealing with a breakup
- you feel alone because everyone in your life has seemingly forgotten that you exist and suddenly remember you when they need something from you
- One of your pets is experiencing pain and you are unable to get to the vet because of circumstances so instead, you take on their pain and beg for healing...*May I just say that this is something a friend tried and the very next day her dog turned a corner and continued getting better*

Angel Nathaniel

Angel Nathaniel is believed to bring purpose to our lives. With a name that means "gift of God," it is not difficult to see why angel mediums would believe this. Some people think that angel Nathaniel is that little voice that tells you which fork in the road to take or to gently shove you to follow the road less traveled. He gives us choices because he wants us to be filled with joy, experience happiness, fall in love, and be guided by the lights that brighten the skies when realizing our passion in life. Angel Nathaniel wants us to excel in life and he is patiently fluttering around while waiting for us to want his help.

Another part of angel Nathaniel's divine tasks is to heal and protect the environment, which includes all living organisms. The more I read about this happy-go-lucky angel, the more I want to meet and spend time with him. I believe that angel Nathaniel's presence will nudge me and whoever he comes in contact with to want to be *that* person who reaches out to help others in need. He is *that* feel-good angel that will not hesitate to play the guilt trip card. I can already see myself offering to babysit the neighbor's screaming children to give their overtired mother a break. Or, he will have me stepping outside of my comfort zone to volunteer to serve lunch at the community soup kitchen.

Angel Nathaniel will keep us humble and grounded so that we will always remember our roots. He will make sure to remind us that reaping all the benefits of his gifts will be lost if we don't spread the love with others. I heard one of the researchers tell their child something that made me smile and realize that this is something everyone could adapt to their lifestyle: "sharing is caring and caring is sharing your love with someone who forgot to find their happy heart." We don't know what someone else is going through, so share your kindness and if you are the one in need of assistance—stick your pride in your back pocket and ask!

I think it is safe to say that angel Nathaniel is one of THOSE angels that should have a whole chapter to himself. Please call on angel Nathaniel when you need help in any of the areas that have been referred to in this section. I hope angel Nathaniel will bless you with just enough of everything you need so that you can keep that fountain flowing.

Angel Ramaela

I recently watched a YouTube video clip by a lady who does angel readings. The moment she drew angel Ramaela's card, her face lit up and she was excited. She also mentioned that she had never drawn her card before, which I believe makes it even more special.

Angel Ramaela is referred to as the angel of joy and laughter. You may recall that you were introduced to archangel Haniel in the previous section, who is also known as the angel of joy. Do you recall me sharing a vision about how angels are handed their daily assignments by the various archangels? I believe that angel Ramaela is one of archangel Haniel's helpers, and she must spread joy and laughter. Imagine being in the company of a grumpy person. Nothing you can say or do can change their perspective on life. Everything is negative, nothing is right, and everyone is doomed. Inspiration hits you and you whip out a smile, add in a drop of humor, a cup of laughter, and you have a recipe that the angels of joy had envisioned for that day. Smiles, laughter, and happiness are infectious and all it takes is one feather kiss to touch the soul of someone who has been too afraid to sparkle.

Angel Ramaela wants you to know that you are allowed to experience happiness and joy, and that laughter is the best medication for any illness. You and I both know that we are living in trying times where the world seems to have lost sense of its faculties because of a global pandemic. That pandemic swept in, caught everyone with their pants around their ankles, and robbed them of their ability to be carefree. Unfortunately, the pandemic will never leave entirely and will at some point be an endemic which, although less severe, is still a reminder of its presence among us.. Does that mean that you aren't allowed to laugh and be happy? Come on, I am daring you to let angel Ramaela come and tickle you with her feathers until you laugh so hard that you end up crying.

I'm not going to give you suggestions of why you would need to call angel Ramaela. I believe that I have said everything that she stands for and what value she adds to our lives. Please remember to send a review to her boss when your soul has been kissed by her feathers.

Angel Sachiel

The name Sachiel means "the covering of God." It is believed that angel Sachiel is part of the Cherubim angels who are located in the first sphere of the celestial hierarchy. In Chapter 1, we learned that the Cherubim angels were tasked to protect the Garden of Eden after Adam and Eve were expelled. They are also in direct contact with God, who gives them the authority to distribute messages and tasks to lower-ranking angels. Angel Sachiel is the angel of wealth, water, success, and prosperity. I was a little startled when I looked at his divine business card and felt as if he was going against the grain of everything I have been researching; but then it dawned on me that I was misinterpreting the business card. Everything I have touched on in this book has been about appreciating what you have, knowing your limits, having a healthy balance, and not being greedy. Angel Sachiel's business card is merely an indication of what he is capable of doing for us. He wants to help us achieve the best version of ourselves that we possibly can. He won't give us more than we can handle, but just enough to help us be comfortable.

The angel mediums believe that he is an upbeat and energetic spiritual being who spreads love, hope, inspiration, caring, healing, and all things positive to all who call on him for guidance. It is no surprise that angel Sachiel would want to try to obliterate all negative energy that surrounds you and brings on mental and physical health concerns. His name, "the covering of God," is an indication of what his heavenly occupation is—he wants to envelop everyone with God's love (or whichever deity you believe in).

Call on angel Sachiel when:
- you are experiencing financial difficulties and need guidance on how to proceed with the situation you are in
- someone approaches you for help with a financial situation and you need guidance to gauge if the request for assistance is real

- you find yourself struggling to claw your way out of the dark maze of depression because you are uncertain about your future

Fallen Angels

The time has come for me to introduce you to the archangels and angels that didn't quite fit the brief to be part of the celestial hierarchy. It is true that everyone lived together in their respective spheres. Everyone respected their positions and worked together to maintain peace and harmony. I think that everyone went about their days by doing what they always had, which was protecting, guiding, and caring for the people, animals, and plant life. God had a well-structured group of spiritual beings who He trusted to carry out His instructions.

No one knows when or how, but it is believed that one of those high-level angels decided that he wasn't happy in the position he was in. He began rallying the angels against each other and built himself a little army. I can only imagine what God was thinking while watching this happen. I like to think that He gave him the rope that he needed to hang himself, but that's just my opinion. Everyone is given a life raft where they are given the opportunity to change their ways and to repair the damage they have created. Unfortunately, not everyone grabs hold of the life raft and they happily kick it so that it floats away faster.

I suspect that the ringleader of the fallen angels wasn't happy being second in command, which is why he recruited his army to commit sins—participate in rebellious acts—and encourage blasphemy against God. I have been struggling to wrap my mind around the idea of not being happy with being an angel. I would love to be an angel without worrying about being hurt, getting sick, or dying. I do wonder if God had a frown while watching the new army of angels being formed and waiting for them to realize that whatever they were planning would not work out too well for them. Remember, I previously mentioned that I believed that God knows what we are thinking, doing, and saying before we even think about it.

I would like to add a disclaimer here that this is a difficult section for anyone who struggles with their spirituality or faith. I want you to feel comfortable and free at all times, and I am still not going to force you to believe anything you don't want to. I have had personal experiences where even considering taking a walk on the other side of the tracks can open one up for some spiritual attacks. Please feel free to call on your angels for protection and surround yourself with the air of positivity. Feel your angels as they swirl around you in preparedness for the last leg of our spiritual journey together.

My Understanding of Fallen Angels

Everyone has an opinion or a thought about everything that happens on earth or in heaven, and one of those opinions has to be the origin of the fallen angels. I want to take a little step back, then a giant leap, and stop when we were children. I don't want to say that everyone had the same experience growing up, but some of us may have had similar experiences. You may or may not have been an unruly child when you were growing up—I believe that the term they use in modern times is attention deficit disorder (ADD) or attention deficit hyperactivity disorder (ADHD). What I am trying to point out is that, at some stage during our formative years, we were told that God is always watching us. If you were misbehaving, you were told that God would put a black dot next to your name; and the day you die, God will look at the list and decide whether you are going to heaven with the angels or to hell with the fallen angels. We were all programmed to think and act in a certain way based on what we were taught growing up. I met many people during my research who shared their stories about growing up in fear. They found themselves second-guessing everything they did until such time that they either started going to church and attended Sunday school or youth groups. Some were too afraid to go to church, and they started researching to understand what they had been told.

I'll just leave a note here for all parents and parents to be: it is never a good idea to make up stories to get your children to cooperate with you. Always be honest with them because they are pretty sharp.

I believe that I have been open with you throughout this book, and I have not forced my views on you. Everyone has to make their own decisions, and if you have learned anything from the angels, you would have seen that they wait on you to ask for guidance. I may have shared my beliefs and opinions, and I will continue sharing them because they are what I believe. I may have found many of the angels very exciting and you can easily spot this in my descriptions of them. I have not, nor will I ever, paint any pictures to deceive you or entice you to follow the course I have set for myself.

I have stated that this chapter is going to be a difficult one. You may learn some things that you do not believe, agree with, or understand. I don't want to get into a spiritual battle about who is right or who is wrong, because that is not what this book is about. We are here to learn about angels and whether they are real or not. Some would say that I should skip through the 'bad' angels and only focus on the good. I believe in balance, and I believe it is important to know who the 'enemy' is and why they are in the position they are in. Knowing this information could educate us to share our knowledge with our angels in order to prevent them from following the same wonky path. It may even help you remain grounded and know that you are not above any law on earth or in heaven. Let's meet these fallen angels...

Meeting the Fallen Angels

I am going to be introducing you to a couple of angels who were expelled from heaven because of their crimes against the Creator of the universe, God. We know that all angels in heaven reside in one of three spheres. One of the angels is rumored to have been a Cherubim. In Chapter 1, you learned that Cherubim angels occupy the second place in the first sphere. You also learned that Cherubim angels were gatekeepers to the Garden of Eden where Adam and Eve lived. Everyone knows the story of Adam and Eve, and what led to their expulsion from the Garden of Eden. It is believed that the serpent, who convinced Eve to eat the forbidden fruit from the Tree of Life, was the leader instigator who started his mission of discrediting God.

Genesis 3:5 tells us: "For God knows that when you eat from it, your eyes will be opened, and you will be like God, knowing good and evil." This is the first indication where the devil was believed to have sinned by lying about God's intention behind the warning about eating the forbidden fruit.

Fast forward to Revelation 12 where you learn about a war in heaven. It is ultimately a power struggle between good and evil where Satan and his followers want to overthrow God as the ruler of the world. It is then that the archangel Michael speaks for the first time in the Bible and says four words as he takes Satan down and they tumble to the earth: "The Lord rebuke you!" It is then believed that one-third of the heavenly angels join Satan on earth. Archangel Michael returns to heaven, in what I believe is his reward for his part in taking Satan down. It is from that day that they were known as and labeled as fallen angels, disgraced angels, or demons. These entities are believed to be moving among the humans on earth today and prompting people to adopt the many sinful acts for which they were expelled.

The Devil

This fallen angel goes by many names. He is a charmer for sure, and the names he goes by are: the devil, Satan, Lucifer, and the prince of evil spirits. He can change his personality to manipulate any situation. I like to think of him as being the self-appointed ruler of the underworld or hell, because those that left heaven with him were too afraid to argue about leadership. I also believe that he was an entitled spiritual being who didn't like being told what to do and when to do it. Today he finds himself ruling the underworld because he didn't believe that rules applied to him.

The devil was cast from heaven before humans were created. This would make sense when you go back to the Adam and Eve scenario and you see that he is believed to have taken on the form of the serpent to speak to and tempt Eve. Nowhere in the Bible do we hear about the devil appearing in human form, which may lead us to believe that angels really don't have human bodies. At best, I like to believe that we use our imaginations to create visuals of what angels—either good or bad—look like. It would make sense if someone told you that they believe archangel Gabriel appeared to them and he looked like Brad Pitt and someone else says that archangel Gabriel appeared to them and that he looked like John Stamos. I know people who have walked where angels fear to walk. They shared their visual images of the devil, and their visions varied from night and day. One said that the devil was the most beautiful and radiant being they had ever seen. Another said that what they saw scared them because he appeared to them looking like a dog with fangs longer than fingers and three horns protruding from his head.

It is not my intention to scare any or conjure up any unnecessary visions, but it is important to know that not everyone sees the same things. I don't believe that the devil wants to scare us, but he does use scare tactics to get our attention. He is the master of deception and hey, if he can sweet talk Eve into believing that God was being selfish by keeping all future knowledge to himself because of personal gain, he is capable of doing anything.

Not everyone is on the same page when it comes to good and evil or angels and demons. Some religions believe that the devil is the reason for the chaos that is happening in the world. Others believe that we are responsible for the chaos we live in. I believe that the devil is a factor in my daily life. I don't wake up in the morning and decide that today is a good day to kick the cat just because it's in my way. That seed of thought had to be planted by someone or something. You are free to believe what you want. I have always told people that you can do whatever you want, but remember that whatever you do has a consequence. The consequence depends on you, and it can be good or it can be bad, so choose wisely.

The Former Angel

Having grown up in the church and being involved in the youth ministry, I had heard many pastors talk about the devil with awe. Mostly because he had the world at his feet—but because of vanity and greed, he wanted more power. We know that the devil was an angel because when we take a look at Ezekiel 28:14, it says: "You were anointed as a guardian cherub, for so I ordained you. You were on the holy mount of God; you walked among the fiery stones." Ezekiel 28:16 says: "Through your widespread trace you were filled with violence, and you sinned. So I drove you in disgrace from the mount of God, and I expelled you, guardian cherub, from among the fiery stones." Scripture shows us that he was part of the Cherubim angels.

He is also referred to as being the most beautiful angel, and again we turn to scripture for confirmation of just how perfect he was. Ezekiel 28:12–13 says: "The Lord says: You were the seal of perfection, full of wisdom and perfect in beauty. You were in Eden, the garden of God; every precious stone adorned you: carnelian, chrysolite and emerald, topaz, onyx and jasper, lapis lazuli, turquoise and beryl. Your settings and mountings were made of gold; on the day you were created they were prepared."

This reminds me of those of us who are not happy with what we have and our need for more perfection, money, or glory. We have everything we could ever want, but because of greed, we lose everything in the blink of an eye. This is exactly what happened to the angel who had everything laid out before him on a silver platter. Ezekiel 28:17–19 shows us how quickly your life can be turned upside down: "Your heart became proud on account of your beauty, and you corrupted your wisdom because of your splendor. So, I threw you to the earth; I made a spectacle of you before kings. By your name since and dishonest trade you have desecrated your sanctuaries. So, I made a fire come out from you, and it consumed you, and I reduced you to ashes on the ground in the sight of all who were watching. All the nations who knew you are appalled at you; you have come to a horrible end and will be no more."

This, my friends, is just one of the accounts of how the devil was 'politely' escorted off the heavenly plain because of greed, sin, and blasphemy against his creator. His obsession with his vanity, and his greed for position and power, blinded him because all he wanted and desired was to be like God so that one day he would be God. I don't know about you, but I think this was not a very wise decision for someone who had everything we all desire—and he ends up losing everything because of greed. Maybe this should be a reminder to everyone that you should be happy with yourself the way you are, because you were created in God's image and in His eyes: you are perfect.

Moloch

The name Moloch is translated from Hebrew and means "king." Moloch was a pagan deity who practiced and encouraged the sacrifice of children. He is also mentioned in the Bible in Leviticus 18:21, where it says: "Do not give any of your children to be sacrificed to Molek, for you must not profane the name of your God. I am the Lord." As you may have noticed, Moloch has various spellings which include Molek and Molech.

Artistic representations of Moloch may have you running for the hills and too afraid to return. I do believe that we don't have to be afraid, though, because our army of angels will keep us safe. They want to protect us, but we have to allow them to do this and not take matters into our own hands. I know what it is like to want to be in control of everything. Unfortunately, life has other plans and ideas, and it is best to hand over the reins and allow your angels to take control. Artists have created the impression that Moloch has a bull-shaped head on the body that resembles a human body—but is not one. His open arms are stretched out as if he is reaching for something. Beneath his outstretched arms, a fire is raging.

An idol of Moloch was created which is rumored to have had seven chambers. One of those chambers was said to be where children were sacrificed. Moloch had a cult-like following which is why the idol was constructed in the Hinnom Valley at Topheth which is outside of Jerusalem. God made his feelings clear about what he thought about the worship of idols and the sacrifices of humans. It is no wonder that Moloch joined the ranks of the fallen angels. He encouraged his followers to build an idol and he invited people to sacrifice their children. Who did he think he was? Did he think he was God who told Abraham to sacrifice his son?

Here you have it, friends—if you believe you are like God, you too will be struck down. Only God can be God. Satan believed he could be God by being a smarty pants and deceiving others, and look where that got him. Moloch thought he could be God by making people sacrifice their children. I think it is safe to assume that it didn't work too well for him.

Chemosh

This fallen angel is believed to have been the national god of Moab. His name is believed to mean "destroyer," "fish god," or "subduer." Scripture leads us to believe that Chemosh was also affiliated with the Ammonites, and Judges 11:23–24 confirms this: "Now since the Lord, the God of Israel, has driven the Amorites out before his people Israel, what right have you to take it over? Will you not take what your god Chemosh gives you? Likewise, whatever the Lord our God has given us, we will possess."

It would seem that King Solomon didn't use the gifts that were bestowed upon him for good. His errors in judgment stacked up and he continued disobeying God's commandments. It is no secret that he was a very wise man who shared his wisdom with all who went to see him, but he did fall short when he became foolish by sinning. King Solomon started worshiping idols and his desire to want more led him to Chemosh. He invited Chemosh and his followers to live in Jerusalem. King Solomon even went as far as to build a temple for them. The temple (or shrine) was eventually broken down by King Josiah 400 years later.

Chemosh is believed to be the one who led the Moabites to victory over their war with the Israelites. Historians have made mention of the Moabite Stone, which mentions Chemosh in glowing terms for his part in the war. The Moabite Stone is a monument and pays tribute to Chemosh. It is also believed that his name appears on the monument a total of 12 times. There was mention that Chemosh wanted to rebuild Moab, but he ran out of time. Chemosh's crime against humanity seems to mirror that of Moloch's.

The Bible verse 2 Kings 3:26–27 shows us the type of person Chemosh was in his human form: "When the king of Moab saw that the battle had gone against him, he took with him seven hundred swordsmen to break through the king of Edom, but they failed. Then he took his firstborn son, who was to succeed him as king, and offered him as a sacrifice on the city wall. The fury against Israel was great; they withdrew and returned to their own land." It is believed that after Chemosh's passing, his followers visited his shrine where they offered up human sacrifices in his honor.

These stories cannot be made up. Whether you are a believer or not, I have to share the evidence from the scriptures about these fallen angels. I am presenting you with what I read and what I have envisioned. If you didn't know that this book was about angels and getting to know the ins and outs, you would most likely have thought that you were reading a script from one of the thrillers on the big screen.

Dagon

The next stop on our fallen angel tour takes us to Dagon. The Philistines named him the West Semitic god of crop fertility or the god of water and grain. He was also believed to have been the god of the

Philistines. He is rumored to have been named as the ruler of the Philistines after the death of King Saul. Thankfully King Saul could choose his manner of death after seeing his sons being killed in the battle between the Philistines and Israel. The verse 1 Chronicles 10:4 reads: "Saul said to his armor-bearer, 'Draw your sword and run me through, or these uncircumcised fellows will come and abuse me.' But his armor-bearer was terrified and would not do it; so Saul took his own sword and fell on it." This was the actions of a brave man because he knew what Dagon and his followers would do if they had to have ended his life.

Verse 1 Chronicles 10:8–10 gives us an indication of what would have happened to King Saul had he been captured alive: "The next day, when the Philistines came to strip the dead, they found Saul and his sons fallen on Mount Gilboa. They stripped him and took his head and his armor, and sent messengers throughout the land of the Philistines to proclaim the news among their idols and their people. They put his armor in the temple of their gods and hung up his head in the temple of Dagon."

Artists have depicted Dagon as being half fish and half man. In modern-day terms, it is believed that he would look like a merman with the top half of his body being human and the bottom of his body being a colorful arrangement of colors and sparkles. Dagon caused a lot of trouble during his reign of terror. He met his end eventually, after attempting to mock God. The story, according to 1 Samuel 5, tells you that the Philistines captured the Ark of the Covenant from Ebenezer and took it to Ashdod. When they got to Ashdod, they placed it in Dagon's temple. They clearly didn't know what they were doing, because the next morning, they got to the temple and Dagon's idol was on the ground where it had toppled over onto his face. His followers restored the idol to its position. The following morning when they returned, they were met with a similar picture, but the difference this time was that Dagon's head and hands had been severed during the fall and were placed at the threshold of the temple.

Naturally, the Ark of the Covenant was removed and returned to its rightful place. The Philistines thought that they were being clever, but they met their match when God entered the arena. You don't have to believe my account of what transpired—and no, I am still not trying to force anyone into a corner about choosing a religion. I am only sharing what I have learned—as I have mentioned many times. I believe that the count of fallen angels is now standing at four—each having believed that they outsmarted the creator of the universe though all have literally fallen short remaining the victor of their crimes.

Belial

Belial is a confusing character. Research had me going around in circles trying to piece it all together only to start over in frustration. The confusion steps in when trying to understand whether Belial was real or just a name that appeared in the Bible or other religious literature. The name Belial means "worthless."

The Old Testament denotes that the word Belial is an indication or a referral to all things evil, bad, or negative. The King James Version of Judges 19:22 tells us: "Now as they were making their hearts merry, behold, the men of the city, certain sons of Belial, beset the house round about, and beat at the door, and spoke to the master of the house, the old man saying, bring forth the man that came into thine house, that we may know him." And when we look at the New International Version (NIV) of the same verse it tells us: "While they were enjoying themselves, some of the wicked men of the city surrounded the house. Pounding on the door, they shouted to the old man who owned the house, 'Bring out the man who came to your house so we can have sex with him'."

The New Testament has one believing that Belial is an actual being as is seen in 2 Corinthians 6:15: "What harmony is there between Christ and Belial? Or what does a believer have in common with an unbeliever?" And then we have religions who believe that Belial is likened to Satan and did indeed fall from heaven with Satan and his merry band of demons.

I believe that the scriptures that I have shared are an indication of who or what Belial is. Whether he was real or only a word to describe evil or denote negativity against a person's character is confusing. Maybe, just maybe, Belial was acting like Satan because he saw that he had a following. An "anything you can do; I can do better" type of scenario. We know that the devil was cunning and knew how to manipulate Eve by making her believe that God was being selfish by not wanting them to have the knowledge. I like to think that as clever as Satan believes he may be, that he is just a mime artist who copies the actions of others that are greater than him. I happen to know many people who do the same by wanting to be who they are not and even going as far as to change their appearances and purchase the same clothing and makeup to look like their influencer. I do believe that Satan (and Belial) do the same and they may succeed in fooling people, but eventually, they get called (or caught) out and their plans fall to the ground.

Beelzebub

The final leg of our "meet the fallen angels" journey is going to be the introduction to Beelzebub. Here we have another fallen angel who is believed to be yet another name for Satan. True or false? I'll let you be the judge because I have concluded that everyone wants to be like Satan. After all, he was not afraid to deceive God. I like to believe that he had many chances to redeem himself, but he was a sneaky angel. I think that Satan didn't like to get his hands dirty and that is why he had everyone else doing his dirty work for him. And this is, where I believe, Beelzebub (and possibly Belial) comes into play.

The name Beelzebub means "lord of the flies" and the Hebrew translation means "lord of dung," or "lord of filth." Artist representation of Beelzebub has him depicted as a fly or as a bat-like creature with wings and a long tail. This disgraced angel is not as prominently mentioned in the scriptures as the others have been, but I don't believe we should dismiss his atrocities against the nations.

It is believed that Beelzebub may have been part of the human sacrifices to idols and that it was his job to ward off the flies. It would make sense that he would be the one tasked with keeping flies away, especially if he is the "lord of the flies." Some theologians believe that

Beelzebub was an exorcist, but instead of driving the bad out of someone, he was tasked with inserting evil into unsuspecting people.

From the research I have done, I have concluded that God was right to have expelled Beelzebub along with the other defying angels. Some believe that hell is a mirror of what heaven looks like. Everything is bright, beautiful, and colorful in heaven; while everything is dark, dreary, and hot in hell. Satan so badly wanted to be like God that when he was expelled—he became the god of the underworld. As God has his three spheres and nine types of angels, so Satan has his demons. Where God has archangel Michael, Satan has Beelzebub doing his dirty work.

Satan takes great pleasure in trying to deceive Christians. It is believed that Satan gives Beelzebub instructions on how to recruit followers, and one such way is having people worshiping false gods. This may be an unpopular belief, but as I see it, these false gods can present in many forms which range from being addicted to pornography, drugs, smoking, or drinking alcohol to committing adultery, murder, theft, or jealousy

-

Conclusion

Our journey together has run its course, and I am preparing you for the landing. Take a deep breath in through your nose and hold for five counts and exhale slowly through your mouth. Now I would like for you to imagine that you are floating above your seat. You feel as if you have developed some magical powers that allow this levitation to occur, but when you squint your eyes you can see something around you.

Honestly Asked and Answered

I asked you to have an open mind throughout this journey. I wanted you to have a little bit of trust and believe that you are not alone. I issued many disclaimers and made as many promises that you would be safe from judgment, condemnation, or bullying. I said that this book was not going to force you to join a specific religion and neither was it going to judge your beliefs or lack thereof. I have a moral obligation to you, the readers, to keep my promises because you are the ones who will share this journey with others.

You may have tried to find the cult sign-up links or the fundamentalist church sign-up links that have been embedded between the descriptions of the angels or even in the Bible verses that I have shared. You are either mildly disappointed to prove that such links don't exist, or hugely relieved to have your assumption about this book being wrong. Either way, you made it this far—and look, we are nearing the end.

I asked you a couple of questions when we set out on this journey together. Let's take a look at the questions again and answer them as honestly as possible. Please join me in answering the questions and comparing your answers.

Are Angels Real?

Yes, I believe that angels are real.

What Leads You to Believe that Angels are Real?

I also believe that the sounds I hear, the smell of my favorite fragrances such as perfumes, baked goods, or flowers, or the relocation of items that occur when no one is or has been in my home are the angels letting me know that they are there. And, I also believe that the angels reach out to me when I am going through a hard time.

Do You Believe in Angels?

Absolutely yes, I do believe in angels. The previous two questions are evidence that I do. Any doubt I previously had has been obliterated.

Why Do You Believe in Angels?

I learned, just like you, while I was writing this book that I am never alone. I may have done my research ahead of time, but I experienced a feeling of total serenity while writing about the angels. The biggest confirmation for me that angels are real and therefore my belief in them, is when I was researching and writing about the fallen angels. I believe, without a shadow of doubt in my mind, that my angels wrapped me in their wings to protect me from the darkness that the fallen angels bring with them.

Are Angels Important to Your Daily life?

Absolutely!

What Leads You to Believe in the Importance of Angels?

We have learned that the angels and archangels are messengers for God. I have assured you that you don't have to be religious and that it is perfectly fine for you to believe in whichever deity you want. Everyone believes in a higher power, so it would make sense that you would have to answer to someone. In my world, I do believe that angels are important because they create a balance between good and bad, dark and light, and happy and sad.

Okay, so the balances may be off here and there, and we can appreciate that the world in general is slightly skewed because of fear. We can believe this to be true because I know that I'm afraid of what the future holds and I know that many friends and colleagues feel this as well. It is not a sin to be afraid, but we should not be living in fear, and this is where I believe that the angels come into play. They fill us with the hope that everything will work out according to the divine plan. They show us that there is beauty surrounding us when we see the green grass, blossoms on the trees, or the blankets of snow as we glance around us.

I would like you to join me in my world where you can see the good that the angels do and why they are important to our mental and physical health and well-being. We need our angels as much as they need us to need them. Don't be afraid to believe.

A Message of Hope and Encouragement

Dear Friends,

I would like to thank you for joining me on this journey. In a couple of minutes, you will be closing your book after reading the last word. You may not be convinced that angels are real, and that is fine. You should not be afraid to put the signs or messages you receive to the test. Life is not as easy as some may want us to believe, and it is your prerogative to ask questions.

I set out to write this book because I was always reaching out to the angels and asking (sometimes begging) for help and guidance in whatever I was doing. I noticed that different angels have different roles in our lives. I learned how to call on my angels by practicing prayer and meditation. I have given you ideas of what you could ask your angels for in your Angel Guide. Don't despair if the angel you need is not mentioned in your Angel Guide. All you have to do is enter meditation or prayer and state the problem you are having and ask for assistance. Your angel will arrive and they will help you with whatever you need.

I don't know what you are going through in your life. Everyone has a journey they need to follow to find the one that suits them. No one should rush you or make the decisions for you. Your parents or guardians guided you through your formative years, and through the years your wants and needs were developed. Life is not easy and it can toss you a couple of wicked curveballs, and this is where I believe that our angels want to be part of our lives. I also believe that this is where they begin leaving messages and signs to let us know that they are around.

If and when you are ready to accept a helping hand from your angels, you can reach up and call on them for whatever (within reason) you may need. Whether you need guidance, assistance, or a touch of internal peace, they are ready to be there for you. Remember your manners when speaking to your angels. *Please* and *thank you* are the magic words to put a smile on your heart and face. Don't be impatient when asking your angels for help, and stop dwelling in the past. You will never be able to go back into the past to change what has been done. However, you can learn from the past and build a better future.

I would like to invite you to read my book, *Angel Numbers 1–9 Meaning: How To Understand the Divine Messages Angels Are Showing You for Twin Flames, Grief, Love, Change, Lost Loved Ones, Friends*. May both of these books lead you to a place where you find angel peace and happiness.

Until we meet again. Stay peaceful, calm, and safe.

References

Ancestry. *Ariel name meaning & Ariel family history.* (n.d.). Ancestry.com. https://www.ancestry.com/name-origin?surname=ariel

Anglin, E. (2020, January 30). *Need legal advice from the angels? Archangel Raziel is your go-to guy.* Learn Religions. https://www.learnreligions.com/archangel-raziel-1728694

Ashcraft, J. (2021, April 8). *Who was Molech in the Bible?.* Christianity.com. https://www.christianity.com/wiki/angels-and-demons/who-was-moloch-in-the-bible.html

Babynology. *Jeremiel meaning, what does Jeremiel name meaning in Christian.* (n.d.). Babynology. https://www.babynology.com/god-goddess-jeremiel_christian.html

Bailey, M. (n.d.). *How angels can help you.* Beliefnet. https://www.beliefnet.com/inspiration/angels/how-angels-can-help-you.aspx

Baines, W. (n.d.). *The spheres of the Christian angelic hierarchy.* Beliefnet. https://www.beliefnet.com/inspiration/angels/the-spheres-of-the-christian-angelic-hierarchy.aspx

Beckler, M. (n.d.-a). *Archangel Sachiel ~ The archangel of wealth, success, and water.* Ask-Angels. https://www.ask-angels.com/spiritual-guidance/archangel-sachiel

Beckler, M. (n.d.-b). *5 Ways to ask for help from the angels*. Ask-Angels. https://www.ask-angels.com/spiritual-guidance/help-from-angels

Biblegateway. (1993). *BibleGateway.com: A searchable online bible in over 150 versions and 50 languages*. BibleGateway. https://www.biblegateway.com

Bolinger, H. (2020a, July 9). *Who is Belial in the Bible?*. Christianity.com. https://www.christianity.com/wiki/christian-terms/who-is-belial.html

Bolinger, H. (2020b, December 10). *Who was Dagon, the philistine fish deity?*. Christianity.com. https://www.christianity.com/wiki/cults-and-other-religions/who-was-dagon-the-philistine-fish-deity.html

The Bump. *Azrael - Baby name meaning, origin and popularity*. (n.d.). The Bump. https://www.thebump.com/b/azrael-baby-name

The Bump. *Haniel - Baby name meaning, origin and popularity*. (n.d.). The Bump. https://www.thebump.com/b/haniel-baby-name

The Bump. *Raziel - Baby name meaning, origin and popularity*. (n.d.). The Bump. https://www.thebump.com/b/raziel-baby-name

The Bump. *Uriel - Baby name meaning, origin and popularity*. (n.d.). The Bump. https://www.thebump.com/b/uriel-baby-name

The Bump. *Zadkiel - Baby name meaning, origin and popularity*. (n.d.). The Bump. https://www.thebump.com/b/zadkiel-baby-name

Burton, J. H. (2019, August 7). *Chemosh: Ancient god of Moabites*. Learn Religions. https://www.learnreligions.com/chemosh-lord-of-the-moabites-117630

Compelling Truth. *Who was Chemosh in the Bible?* (n.d.). Compelling Truth. https://www.compellingtruth.org/who-Chemosh.html

Cossetta, E. (2018, April 24). *9 Types of angels you should know about*. Thought Catalog. https://thoughtcatalog.com/erin-cossetta/2018/04/9-types-of-angels-you-should-know-about

Dee. (2014, March 10). *Angel Amatiel ~ Hope*. Archangel Oracle. https://archangeloracle.com/2014/03/10/angel-amatiel-hope

Dee. (2017, June 29). *Ramaela ~ Joy*. Archangel Oracle. https://archangeloracle.com/2017/06/29/ramaela-joy

Demers, D. (n.d.). *The 7 archangels and their meanings*. Beliefnet. https://www.beliefnet.com/inspiration/angels/galleries/the-7-archangels-and-their-meanings.aspx

Dictionary.com. *Definition of Raphael*. (n.d.). Dictionary.com. https://www.dictionary.com/browse/raphael

Dreamer. (n.d.). *7 Signs your guardian angels is trying to contact you*. LoveThisPic. https://www.lovethispic.com/blog/15186/7-signs-your-guardian-angel-is-trying-to-contact-you

The Editors of Encyclopaedia Britannica. (n.d.). *Moloch | Definition & Facts*. Encyclopedia Britannica. https://www.britannica.com/topic/Moloch-ancient-god

Encyclopædia Britannica. *Chemosh | Semitic deity | Britannica*. (n.d.). Encyclopædia Britannica. https://www.britannica.com/topic/Chemosh

Encyclopædia Britannica. *Dagan | Semitic god | Britannica*. (n.d.). Encyclopædia Britannica. https://www.britannica.com/topic/Dagan

Encyclopædia Britannica. *Isrāfīl | Islamic mythology*. (n.d.). Encyclopædia Britannica. https://www.britannica.com/topic/Israfil

Fairchild, M. (2020, July 2). *What does the Bible say about angels?*.. Learn Religions. https://www.learnreligions.com/what-does-the-bible-say-about-angels-701965

Fleming, E. (2020, February 26). *Why are angels called thrones?* SidmartinBio. https://www.sidmartinbio.org/why-are-angels-called-thrones/#How_are_Thrones_related_to_the_throne_of_God

Garone, S. (2021, September 26). *Gabriel name meaning* Verywell Family. https://www.verywellfamily.com/gabriel-name-meaning-origin-popularity-5118182

The Goddess Lifestyle Plan. (2013, June 2). *How to call upon your spirit guides and guardian angels*. The Goddess Lifestyle Plan. https://www.goddesslifestyleplan.com/how-to-call-upon-your-spirit-guides-and-guardian-angels

Got Questions. *Who was Belial?* (n.d.). Got Questions. https://www.gotquestions.org/who-Belial.html

Guardian Angel Guide. *Guardian angel Dokiel.* (2017, February 9). Guardian Angel Guide. https://guardianangelguide.com/guardian-angel-dokiel

Hdogar. (2021, May 21). *Lucifer — The fallen angel.* Medium. https://medium.com/lessons-from-history/lucifer-the-fallen-angel-eb788bf728ba

Hluchan, K. T. (2018, March 21). *The archangels and their divine responsibilities.* Hatboro-Horsham, PA Patch. https://patch.com/pennsylvania/horsham/archangels-their-divine-responsibilities

Hooker, A. (2021, March 4). *Why was satan called Beelzebub in the Bible?* Christianity.com. https://www.christianity.com/wiki/angels-and-demons/who-was-beelzebub-in-the-bible.html

Hopler, W. (2017a, March 7). *Angel types in Christianity (The pseudo-dionysius angelic hierarchy).* Learn Religions. https://www.learnreligions.com/angel-types-in-christianity-123833

Hopler, W. (2017b, July 15). *Meet archangel Jophiel, angel of beauty.* Learn Religions. https://www.learnreligions.com/meet-archangel-jophiel-124094

Hopler, W. (2017c, July 15). *Meet archangel Sandalphon, angel of music.* Learn Religions. https://www.learnreligions.com/meet-archangel-sandalphon-124089

Hopler, W. (2018a, March 31). *Meet archangel Uriel, angel of wisdom.* Learn Religions. https://www.learnreligions.com/meet-archangel-uriel-angel-of-wisdom-124717

Hopler, W. (2018b, April 1). *Meet archangel Ariel, the angel of nature.* Learn Religions. https://www.learnreligions.com/archangel-ariel-the-angel-of-nature-124074

Hopler, W. (2018c, April 15). *Archangel Jeremiah's roles and symbols.* Learn Religions. https://www.learnreligions.com/meet-archangel-jeremiel-124080

Hopler, W. (2018d, July 28). *Archangel Zadkiel, the angel of mercy.* Learn Religions. https://www.learnreligions.com/meet-archangel-zadkiel-124092

Hopler, W. (2018e, August 25). *Archangel Azrael.* Learn Religions. https://www.learnreligions.com/meet-archangel-azrael-124093

Hopler, W. (2019a, January 3). *How to recognize archangel Haniel.* Learn Religions. https://www.learnreligions.com/how-to-recognize-archangel-haniel-124304

Hopler, W. (2019b, January 20). *How to recognize archangel Uriel.* Learn Religions. https://www.learnreligions.com/how-to-recognize-archangel-uriel-124286

Hopler, W. (2019c, January 24). *Signs of the archangel Sandalphon.* Learn Religions. https://www.learnreligions.com/how-to-recognize-archangel-sandalphon-124283

Hopler, W. (2019d, January 30). *How do I recognize archangel Zadkiel?*. Learn Religions. https://www.learnreligions.com/how-to-recognize-archangel-zadkiel-124287

Hopler, W. (2019e, February 10). *How to recognize Archangel Michael*. Learn Religions. https://www.learnreligions.com/how-to-recognize-archangel-michael-124278

Hopler, W. (2019f, January 20). *How to recognize archangel Chamuel*. Learn Religions. https://www.learnreligions.com/how-to-recognize-archangel-chamuel-124273

Hopler, W. (2019g, February 23). *What are angels made of?* Learn Religions. https://www.learnreligions.com/what-are-angels-made-of-123836

Hopler, W. (2019h, April 27). *As the patron saint of healing, Raphael heals body, mind, and spirit*. Learn Religions. https://www.learnreligions.com/saint-raphael-the-archangel-124675

Hopler, W. (2019i, April 28). *What are dominion angels?*. Learn Religions. https://www.learnreligions.com/what-are-dominion-angels-123907

Hopler, W. (2019j, April 29). *How to recognize archangel Barachiel*. Learn Religions. https://www.learnreligions.com/how-to-recognize-archangel-barachiel-124272

Hopler, W. (2019k, April 29). *How to recognize archangel Gabriel.* Learn Religions. https://www.learnreligions.com/how-to-recognize-archangel-gabriel-124274

Hopler, W. (2019l, May 1). *Meet archangel Raguel, angel of justice and harmony.* Learn Religions. https://www.learnreligions.com/meet-archangel-raguel-124086

Hopler, W. (2019m, May 9). *How to recognize archangel Metatron.* Learn Religions. https://www.learnreligions.com/how-to-recognize-archangel-metatron-124277

Hopler, W. (2019n, May 9). *Meet archangel Metatron, angel of life.* Learn Religions. https://www.learnreligions.com/meet-archangel-metatron-124083

Hopler, W. (2019o, June 25). *Archangel Raziel profile.* Learn Religions. https://www.learnreligions.com/meet-archangel-raziel-124087

Hurst, K. (2019, March 26). *14 Common angel symbols and signs to look out for.* The Law of Attraction. https://www.thelawofattraction.com/angel-signs-symbols

Inner Light Sanctum. (2020, November 10). *Angel reading and light activation - Joy with angel Ramaela* [Video]. YouTube. https://www.youtube.com/watch?v=dMcAa7wy_d4

Jenkins, D. (2019, November 8). *Are demons really fallen angels?.* Christianity.com. https://www.christianity.com/wiki/angels-and-demons/are-demons-really-fallen-angels.html

Kranz, J. (2013, November 7). *6 Biblical facts about Michael the archangel.* OverviewBible. https://overviewbible.com/michael-archangel

Kranz, J. (2016, December 22). *11 Fascinating facts about the angel Gabriel.* OverviewBible. https://overviewbible.com/angel-gabriel-facts

Mama Natural. *Azrael.* (n.d.). Mama Natural. https://www.mamanatural.com/baby-names/boys/azrael

Mama Natural. *Barachiel.* (n.d.). Mama Natural. https://www.mamanatural.com/baby-names/boys/barachiel

Mama Natural. *Chamuel.* (n.d.). Mama Natural. https://www.mamanatural.com/baby-names/boys/chamuel

Mama Natural. *Jophiel.* (n.d.). Mama Natural. https://www.mamanatural.com/baby-names/boys/jophiel

Margaritoff, M. (2021, October 6). *The true history of Moloch, the ancient god of child sacrifice.* All That's Interesting. https://allthatsinteresting.com/moloch

Marks, H. (2021, November 5). *Dreams.* WebMD. https://www.webmd.com/sleep-disorders/dreaming-overview

Mbuthia, M. (2020, March 9). Different types of angels and their hierarchy. Legit. https://www.legit.ng/1307665-different-types-angels-hierarchy.html

Meaning of the Name. *Meaning of the name Israfel.* (n.d.). Meaning of the Name. https://www.meaningofthename.com/israfel

Merriam-Webster. *Definition of Archangel.* (n.d.). Merriam-Webster. https://www.merriam-webster.com/dictionary/archangel

Moloch. (n.d.). Wikipedia. https://en.wikipedia.org/wiki/Moloch

Moore, J. D. (2016, July 24). *7 Shocking ways angels speak to you every day.* PsychCentral. https://psychcentral.com/blog/life-goals/2016/07/ways-angels-speak-to-you

Nameberry. *Uriel - Baby name meaning, origin, and popularity.* (n.d.). Nameberry. https://nameberry.com/babyname/Uriel

Padre. (2021a, August 5). *Archangel Haniel - Assist in the best way possible!.* Padre. https://www.guardian-angel-reading.com/blog-of-the-angels/archangel-haniel

Padre. (2021b, December 15). *Sagittarius horoscope and the archangel Raguel.* Padre. https://www.guardian-angel-reading.com/blog-of-the-angels/sagittarius-horoscope

Padre. (2021c, December 15). *Virgo horoscope and the archangel Metatron.* Padre. https://www.guardian-angel-reading.com/blog-of-the-angels/virgo-horoscope

Pearce, J. (2020, March 9). *5 Ways to connect with your guardian angels.* Mindbodygreen. https://www.mindbodygreen.com/0-17567/5-ways-to-connect-with-your-guardian-angel.html

Plant, R. (2021, July 3). *What does the name Michael mean?.* Verywell Family. https://www.verywellfamily.com/michael-name-meaning-5115812

Radford, B. (2018, March 29). *Are angels real?.* Live Science. https://www.livescience.com/26071-are-angels-real.html

Ross, A. (2021, January 15). *5 Comforting facts about archangel Cassiel - Archangel secrets*. Archangel Secrets. https://www.archangelsecrets.com/5-uplifting-facts-archangel-cassiel

The Secret of the Tarot. *Archangel Muriel*. (n.d.). The Secret of the Tarot. https://thesecretofthetarot.com/archangel-muriel

Shelton, J. (2021, September 23). *Meet Beelzebub, who somehow is and isn't the devil*. Ranker. https://www.ranker.com/list/beelzebub-facts/jacob-shelton

Site Master. (n.d.). *Angel Ananchel angel of grace - ask an angel*. Ask an Angel. https://askanangel.org/angel-ananchel-angel-of-grace

Smith, L. (n.d.). *Archangel Nathaniel - The gift of God in our lives*. Sun Signs. https://www.sunsigns.org/archangel-nathaniel-the-gift-of-god-in-our-lives

Standley, L. J. (n.d.). *Ananchel ~ angel of grace: Angels, archangels, guardian angels, holy angels, what are angels?* Drstandley. https://www.drstandley.com/angels_ananchel.shtml

Tanaaz. (n.d.). *11 Things you can call on angels to help you with*. Forever Conscious. https://foreverconscious.com/11-things-can-call-angels-help

Taylor, S. (n.d.-a). *Achaiah is the guardian angel of understanding and communication*. Astrofame. https://my.astrofame.com/clairvoyance/article/achaiah-guardian-angel

Taylor, S. (n.d.-b). *Anauel guardian angel: A symbol of courage and militancy*. Astrofame. https://my.astrofame.com/clairvoyance/article/anauel-guardian-angel

Taylor, S. (n.d.-c). *Aniel, the guardian angel of audacious and determined individuals*. Astrofame. https://my.astrofame.com/clairvoyance/article/aniel-guardian-angel

Taylor, S. (n.d.-d). *Asaliah, the guardian angel who guides you towards the truth*. Astrofame. https://my.astrofame.com/clairvoyance/article/asaliah-guardian-angel

Taylor, S. (n.d.-e). *Cahetel, guardian angel offering blessing and abundance*. Astrofame. https://my.astrofame.com/clairvoyance/article-cahetel-guardian-angel

Taylor, S. (n.d.-f). *Caliel guardian angel, the symbol of justice and truth*. Astrofame. https://my.astrofame.com/clairvoyance/article/caliel-guardian-angel

Taylor, S. (n.d.-g). *Chavaquiah, the guardian angel of reconciliation and harmony*. Astrofame. https://my.astrofame.com/clairvoyance/article/chavaquiah-guardian-angel

Taylor, S. (n.d.-h). *Damabiah guardian angel: Altruism and generosity*. Astrofame.

https://my.astrofame.com/clairvoyance/article/damabiah-guardian-angel

Taylor, S. (n.d.-i). *Daniel, the guardian angel who brings comfort and consolation.* Astrofame. https://my.astrofame.com/clairvoyance/article/daniel-guardian-angel

Taylor, S. (n.d.-j). *Elemiah, guardian angel of success and protection.* Astrofame. https://my.astrofame.com/clairvoyance/article/elemiah-guardian-angel

Taylor, S. (n.d.-k). *Eyael guardian angel: The protector of those born between February 20 - 24.* Astrofame.

Tripple, M. (2020, December 3). *9 Types of angels you should know about.* EverythingMom. https://www.everythingmom.com/parenting/soul/angels-types

Understanding Compassion. (2018, February 13). *7 Signs someone you met is an earth angel.* Understanding Compassion. https://understandingcompassion.com/articles/7-signs-someone-met-earth-angel

Vernon, A. (2018, February 8). *The complete guide to angel Amitiel.* The Seventh Angel Book. https://theseventhangelbook.com/angel-guidance/the-complete-guide-to-angel-amitiel

White, L. (n.d.). *What are the 9 orders of angels?*. Beliefnet. https://www.beliefnet.com/inspiration/angels/what-are-the-9-orders-of-angels.aspx

Wikipedia. *Israfil*. (2022, January 15). Wikipedia.org. https://en.wikipedia.org/wiki/Israfil

Wikipedia. *Zadkiel*. (2022, January 20). Wikipedia.org. https://en.wikipedia.org/wiki/Zadkiel

Wimon. *Jeremiel: What is the meaning of the name Jeremiel? Analysis numerology origin*. (n.d.). Wimon. https://www.whatisthemeaningofname.com/what-is-the-meaning-of-the-name-jeremiel-31417

Wimon. *Raguel: What is the meaning of the name Raguel? Analysis numerology origin*. (n.d.). Wimon. https://www.whatisthemeaningofname.com/what-is-the-meaning-of-the-name-raguel-20550

Wisner, W. (2021, July 2). *Daniel name meaning*. Verywell Family. https://www.verywellfamily.com/daniel-name-meaning-origin-popularity-5115352

Image References

Ball, M. (2020, December 23). [*Man in jacket and pants standing beside black statue*]. Unsplash. [Image]. https://unsplash.com/photos/dSoR8sLMSIE

Birmingham Museums Trust. (2019, December 23). *Night with her Train of Stars, 1912 The painting's title is derived from W. E Henley's (1849-1903) poem 'Margaritae Sorori' (Translates as 'Sister Margaret') Artist: E.R.Hughes (Edward Robert Hughes).* Unsplash. [Image]. https://unsplash.com/photos/JZdPBgU6Nik

Boccardo, L. (2019, June 1). [*Man holding spear statue*]. Unsplash. [Image]. https://unsplash.com/photos/F6uH7WvRwiA

British Library. (2020, March 17). *Valentine's Day - A selection of love inspired images from British Library's digitised 19th Century books.* Unsplash. [Image]. https://unsplash.com/photos/k7Xkq28tFQY

Chystiakov, E. (2021, October 19). *Creepy and beauty.* Unsplash. [Image]. https://unsplash.com/photos/cpjTDY_0dZ4

Curry, C. (2020, April 26). [*Angel statue under which clouds during daytime*]. Unsplash. [Image]. https://unsplash.com/photos/lTkaZlyZFrQ

Geo, A. (2019, October 29). *Michael Angelo's painting on top of the Palace of Versailles.* Unsplash. [Image]. https://unsplash.com/photos/1rBg5YSi00c

Huang, X. (2021, January 31). [*Woman in white dress statue*]. Unsplash. [Image]. https://unsplash.com/photos/r4YqNJ1QR_U

Javardh. (2018, May 26). [*Shallow focus photography of white feather dropping in person's hand*]. Unsplash. [Image]. https://unsplash.com/photos/FL6rma2jePU

Kadel, J. (2020a, May 2). [*Angel statue under white string lights*]. Unsplash. [Image]. https://unsplash.com/photos/PdEsP8rAVY0

Kadel, J. (2020b, May 19). [*Man sitting on rock statue*]. Unsplash. [Image]. https://unsplash.com/photos/a8GewfTgpys

Kuznietsov, V. (2021, November 1). *Canon EOS 4000D Canon EF-S 18-135mm f3.5-5.6 IS ISO 200 | f 5.6 | 1/200s 18MP | 5184x3456.* Unsplash. [Image]. https://unsplash.com/photos/DQEBp8Jq6JI

Miao, Y. (2021, August 12). [*Woman in pink dress holding white feather*]. Unsplash. [Image]. https://unsplash.com/photos/wQKJ9XSd8x8

Rasmussen, K. (2018, April 27). *Sakura festival in copenhagen. Instagram - Kasper.cph.* Unsplash. [Image]. https://unsplash.com/photos/9cl0CpxyYnY

Sanchez, D. (2020, April 18). [*Man in brown jacket and pants holding white umbrella*]. Unsplash. [Image]. https://unsplash.com/photos/sjizej8fY2w

Scarionati, F. (2021, January 14). *Angel in Ponte Sant'Angelo, Rome.* Unsplash. [Image]. https://unsplash.com/photos/EomurrCz3dk

Skirr, R. (2019, December 12). *Angel statue on a graveyard in Kaiserslautern, Germany.* Unsplash. [Image]. https://unsplash.com/photos/5WWkAYZgw7U

Studzinski, M. (2019, November 2). *angel, woman, beautiful, nice, lovely, Pretty, breasts, Cemetery, graveyard, mist, fog, gray, grey, Hamburg, Ohlsdorf, green, Body, wings, autumn, Cold, garten, trees, head, dress, gown, death, tomb, grave, Stone*. Unsplash. [Image]. https://unsplash.com/photos/TEZLseYfyz0

Trajan, T. (2021, September 22). [*Free Sihlfeld*]. Unsplash. [Image]. https://unsplash.com/photos/2KOLIUaphJo

Zaccaria, A. (2019, December 8). *Krampus: one of the traditions of South Tyrol (Northern Italy)*. Unsplash. [Image]. https://unsplash.com/photos/po1ffK4lLMw

www.ingramcontent.com/pod-product-compliance
Lightning Source LLC
Chambersburg PA
CBHW070729020526
44107CB00077B/2275